The Pacific Coast

California poppy

photography by **RAY ATKESON**
text by CALVIN KENTFIELD

RAND MᶜNALLY & COMPANY
Chicago   New York   San Francisco

Ecola State Park on the Oregon coast. Haystack Rock is silhouetted in the distant haze on Cannon Beach.

The Pacific Coast

Book Design by Vito DePinto

A fall of water from Ramona Creek veils a cliff
of lava basalt in Oregon's Mt. Hood National Forest.

Mimulus, in Redwood National Park
near the northern California coast.

Contents

Redwood National Park, with flowering rhododendron.

In the Pacific Coast states of California, Oregon, and Washington, the ancient Greek elements of the terrestrial world —air, fire, earth, water—still lie and work deeply in nature: in the mountains and the shoreline, the deserts and fertile valleys, the great rivers and the high plateaus. Of these four elementary things, the last, water, is the primal force; for its abundance or its lack determines the character, the face and features, of this extraordinary region, which comprises 323,866 square miles of the American landscape—a region which in places is incredibly beautiful,

Introduction

Anza-Borrego Desert State Park, almost half a million acres of desert land in southern California.

A California coastal sunset, at Patrick's Point State Park.

in places dangerous and terrifying, in places heartbreakingly ravished, in some places monotonous and tedious, and in some other places weird and grand and even spooky.

Should a crow, a golden eagle, or any other natural, or even man-made, bird fly from Baja California to British Columbia, it would travel 1,310 miles, from the driest to the wettest places on the continent. For instance, two years, one month, and a week went by without a single drop of water falling from the sky at Bagdad, a nearly abandoned gold-mining town with a population of 20, on the old Highway 66 in California's Mojave Desert.

Deer and cypress,
against a sunset on
California's Monterey
Peninsula.

On the horizon beyond
Tule Lake in Northern California
is Mt. Shasta.
The ducks taking off
and the geese in passage
have or will feed and rest at
Tule Lake wildlife refuge.

Shooting star,
also known as bird bill,
in bloom at Devils Postpile
National Monument,
California.

(This is dry, but it hardly compares with the Atacama Desert in northern Chile, where rain has not fallen for at least 400 years.)

On the other hand, 140 inches of rain per year is not uncommon on the western slope of Washington's Olympic Peninsula. In fact, during the winter of 1955-56, Paradise Valley

Pebbles seen at ebb tide on the shore of Point Lobos Reserve, California.

Wild oat grass, in California's
Mother Lode region.

near the timberline of Mt. Rainier, also in Washington State, broke the world's record for the most snow in one season— with nearly 84 feet.

These, of course, are extremes, and the Pacific states are not lacking in other extremes for the continental United States: California has the most people, the lowest land, and the biggest trees; Oregon has the deepest lake and the deepest canyon; and Washington has the wettest place—it also has the largest concrete structure on earth. In addition to extremes, this is a land of striking variety, with marked contrast being the rule rather

Limb of a bristlecone pine, a tree
which grows in groves reaching
12,000 feet in elevation
in California's White Mountains. Some
of the living trees are 4,000 years old.

Dunes at evening in Death Valley
National Monument, California.

than the exception. For example, the little town of Sausalito, on San Francisco Bay, has seven horticulturally recognized climatic regions within its city limits.

There is an unexpected juxtaposition of opposites—fog and sun, high and low, flat and rugged, green and brown, cold and heat, lush and arid, crowded and empty, pure and polluted, wild and tame, and wet and dry. The social and economic contrasts result basically from climatic contrasts, and the differences of climate result by and large from the Pacific Ocean and the water it does or does not bring on the wind.

echnically, southern California is a desert, but rain does fall on the coast in winter so that the really arid deserts lie in the southeast, from Mexico to Death Valley and from the Colorado River to the Tehachapi Mountains (the curved, transverse tail of the Sierra Nevada).

The Anza-Borrego Desert, lying between the jumbled Coast Ranges of San Diego County and the Imperial Valley, is itself a jumble of sere, scrub-covered mountain ranges, cactuses, palm oases, alkali flats, and bare rock. It contains the largest state park in the nation, 488,000 acres of mostly primitive land. There are airports and roads, however, and at Borrego Springs a golf course, which draws water from underground, creating a green oasis in the pink and tawny dust. The mountains possess evocative names—Volcan, for instance, and Oriflamme.

North of Borrego Springs, part of Clarks Dry Lake was used by the University of Maryland a few years ago as the site for a radio telescope with more than two miles of antennae to read those faint and frequently puzzling "messages," the galactic noises from space. (This radio telescope is rather small compared to Jodrell Bank in England or the installation at Chuguyev in the Ukraine, which has a range of more than 10 billion light-years.)

About 35 miles to the west of Clarks Dry Lake, on the top of Palomar Mountain, is the famous 200-inch Hale reflector telescope. It is the largest of its kind on earth (until 1972 when the Russians plan to complete their 236-inch telescope in the towering ranges of the Kirghiz in central Asia). Capable of finding the light of a star with the brilliance of the light of a candle 40,000 miles away, the Hale telescope enables the scientist to see "the known limits of the observable universe." (The large observatories of California are in trouble now because of smog—not so much Palomar, but Mt. Wilson near Los Angeles and particularly San Jose's Lick Observatory, which has almost had to shut down altogether.)

The Anza-Borrego Desert and its mountains, with their vast, starry nights and their contact and "conversation" with the stars, have be-come favorite places for sighting Unidentified Flying Objects, strange lights, and other celestial phenomena having spiritual significance for those people susceptible to such beliefs. More than one earthly human has claimed to have met and spoken with or ridden away and come back to this desert with beings from other planets.

The northeast corner of the Anza-Borrego drops into the Salton Sink, once the location of several prehistoric lakes. Here portions of the earth's crust between two fault lines sank (like the Dead Sea and San Francisco Bay) while mountains rose on either side. The sea moved in, formed lakes that eventually evaporated, leaving shores and terraces, visible today, and oyster shells and fossil shark's teeth imbedded high up on the mountain walls. The Colorado River also, over the ages, laid down mountains of rich silt, damming the head of the Gulf of California and from time to time overflowing into the sink, forming freshwater lakes that too in several hundred years or so of intense heat evaporated, leaving a dry, immense plain at the base of what are now called the Chocolate Mountains, a plain of such alluvial richness that even early visitors to this land of unearthly heat and rainless days could recognize it as a possible blooming garden in the desert.

In 1901 the California Development Company, an enthusiastic but slipshod and irresponsible group of pushers, formed a subsidiary called the Imperial Land Company and renamed that part of the Colorado Desert the Imperial Valley, which was, and of course still is, well below the surface of the sea. The developers built, through Mexico, an irrigation canal meant to tap the prodigious flow of the Colorado River. It did. Water poured in and so did people, by the thousands.

But in 1905, in unseasonable flood, the river did its ancient thing; it overflowed into the valley instead of flowing on to the sea. These millions of tons of water that had, at its sources, tumbled down numberless gorges of the snowy Rockies, picking up the flow of rivers—the Gunnison, the Dolores, the Green, the San Juan—rising on the western slopes of the Continental Divide, rolled through the Grand Can-yon, gathering up, finally, the waters of the Gila, were diverted into the canal, whose steep slope provided a much more amenable course for the flood than the gentler slope of the natural riverbed.

For two years the huge river crossed the valley and "emptied itself," according to the Encyclopaedia Britannica reporting the incident in 1911, "into a great natural depression [Salton Sink] and formed the so-called 'Salton Sea,' about 80 m. long, 20 wide and 100 ft. deep, before it could be brought under control. This sea is now isolated, and will, it is hoped, dry up in eight or ten years." The author of that account, Cleveland Abbe, a meteorologist, went to his grave believing and hoping that the Salton Sea would disappear. It has not, nor is it likely to, because, in spite of the heat of the Imperial Valley (I have experienced temperatures of 112° F. at midnight in El Centro) and the scarcity of rain (three inches a year), this sea without exit—though it, of course, evaporates—is continually fed by the New and Alamo rivers, that in turn are fed by seepage from the miles and miles of canals and irrigation ditches. The mean surface elevation remains much the same—235 feet below sea level—and it has become quite salty, allowing only such fish as mullet, sargo, and corbina to thrive. (How the first fish got into the sea remains a mystery.) Being so shallow (now an average of 40 feet) it can be a rough and treacherous body when the high desert winds rise, so boatmen and fishermen are requested to take care. The shores of the lake have been developed into recreation areas and resorts with motels, marinas, yacht clubs, and winter homes, so nobody wants it to dry up anymore.

Watered by the Colorado River through the All-American Canal, the Coachella Canal, and others, as well as by underground water, the Coachella and Imperial valleys, north and south of the Salton Sea, are among the world's most remarkable food-producing regions. With virtually every day of the year a growing day, up to six full crops a year can be harvested. Those crops include alfalfa, cotton, sugar beets, lettuce, watermelons, cantaloupes, carrots, onions, tomatoes, garlic, grapes, dates, nuts, oranges, and grapefruit.

The main street of the town of Coachella is called Cantaloupe Avenue. Indio, "the date capital of the nation," grows more grapes than dates, but its thoroughfares are lined with tall date palms, some of them very old and very elegant. During the National Date Festival the townsfolk go about in tarbooshes and bangles, dressed like Arabs. Camels are occasionally in evidence.

Up the road from Indio is Palm Springs, around and over and alongside the Agua Caliente Indian Reservation, part of which the Indians have allowed to be developed and part of which they have retained in its natural state. Palm Springs, with its superb warm, dry winter climate, has become the most popular and expensive resort area on the Pacific Coast. However, there have been complaints in recent years that evaporation from the thousands of swimming pools and from the watering of golf courses has dampened the air; and there have been complaints too about a condition new to the pure air of the desert—smog. Its hotels (motel is a dirty word in Palm Springs) may charge as much as $99 a day for a room. Between Palm Springs and Indio there are, at this writing, 19 golf courses, both public and private, and more being planned. Although in the 20 miles from Indio to Palm Springs the land rises from 15 feet below sea level to 458 feet above, this is the low desert.

A few miles to the northeast of Palm Springs lies the Joshua Tree National Monument, approximately 870 square miles of much higher land (1,000 to 6,000 feet in elevation), which makes the transition between the low desert and the high desert of the Mojave. The monument is a native desert preserve with one paved road passing all the way through it from the monument headquarters at Twentynine Palms (a natural oasis) to Interstate 10. Some years ago efforts were made by commercial interests to construct a shortcut highway across the monument to draw into the Coachella Valley the paychecks from the United States Marine Corps Training Center near Twentynine Palms. A successful quietus, however, was effected for this plan by the Desert Protective Council, and as a result, the natural life and landscape remain undisturbed.

The monument is named for the Joshua tree, which is technically not a tree at all, but an enormous lily that sometimes attains 40 feet in height and that bursts forth with white blossoms in the spring. The Mormons named it because of its outstretched limbs. "And the Lord said unto Joshua, Stretch out the spear that is in thy hand toward Ai . . . and Joshua stretched out the spear that he had in his hand toward the city." Perhaps it is the strangest of many a strange plant that has found a way to live, and live long, in the desert.

The Joshua trees, which may survive several hundred years, are not the only inhabitants that ornament the sands and granite and mountains of the monument. There are the ocotillo, or candlewood, a weird aggregation of thin, waving canes, sometimes 20 feet long, encrusted with vicious thorns, and in spring, covered with spectacular scarlet flowers; the spiny, wispy smoke tree, fragrant in June and lively with thrashers and gnatcatchers; cactuses—barrel, cholla, darning-needle, beavertail; the tall, bearded, shade-giving fan palm clustered at oases; and the aromatic creosote bush and sage. There are animals too—the brush-tailed kangaroo rat, the antelope squirrel, the tiny, racing lizard, the fat chuckwalla (the Indians' chicken) lounging in the sun, and the shy desert bighorn sheep of the Hexie and Coxcomb mountains. At night in spring the moon shines bright, a coyote howls, and the sweet scent of sand verbena pervades the starry night. A classical desert.

The Mojave Desert is 2,000 feet high on the average, with peaks up to 7,000 feet. It is 15,000 square miles of sand, sudden mountains, deep gorges, fantastic rocks, dry lake beds, dunes, craters, seas of black lava, cinder cones, Joshua trees, mesquite, lizards, and many other plants and small animals. The Mojave is cooler than the deserts down below, and in fact in winter gets quite cold. Hideously hot in summer with hot winds blowing, it seems a dun and lifeless place, and the desiccated traveler wonders if it will ever end. It's twice as big as New Jersey and half as big as Superior, the largest freshwater lake in the world. It was once a part of the sea, and then a lake; and shells can be found along with the fossil re-

mains of prehistoric mastodons, camels, and horses. Like the sea, it creates its anti-images. Whereas the sailor long on the water may see phantom islands on the vague horizon, the desert wanderer in the shimmering heat will see lakes and sailboats and palm trees or hear the sound of rushing water.

There is a river, the Mojave River, that never goes quite dry. It rises in the San Bernardino Mountains, flows sometimes underground, sometimes through deep canyons it has cut through the granite and limestone ages and disappears into the sand or the slimy playa of dry Soda Lake. The Mojave River valley was part of the Spanish Trail, a heavily traveled path to southern California from Santa Fe. The trail was first used by trappers, such as Jedediah Smith, and other famous men of the West—Kit Carson and John C. Frémont. Now Interstate 15 and the Atcheson, Topeka and Santa Fe and the Southern Pacific railroads follow it a good part of the way toward Las Vegas. There are dry washes too that channel avalanches of water, boulders, and mud onto the desert floor from sudden torrential thunderstorms in distant mountains. The Mojave is an imprisoned desert with no outlet to the sea. When the water comes down or the winter rains fall, the living plants absorb it while they can, and in the spring, the ugly dust and dreary mountains come wondrously alive with birds and scents and blossoms and even green grass. All it takes is water.

The eastern part of the Mojave has few inhabitants, but the western part—from Barstow to the San Bernardino and Tehachapi mountains, south to Twentynine Palms, and north to the Owens Valley—is a booming, rapidly filling region of farming and beef and chicken raising. Also, the aerospace industry has followed the Air Force into this area of vast, flat, hard places that are so suitable for airplanes, and of dry air salubrious for delicate electronic instruments. A look at the map will reveal over twenty private airports, at least three military airfields, and three commercial fields. The longest runway in the world (seven miles) is at Rogers Dry Lake at Edwards Air Force Base. Just over the hills from Los Angeles, this part of the desert is immensely popular for those typically, if not exclusively, southern California sports of auto racing and motorcycling. Recently 2,000 amateur cyclists participated in a race across the Mojave from Barstow to Las Vegas.

The last great desert of California, most of which is a national monument, includes Death Valley and the nearby Panamint Valley. The tales and the legends, and indeed, the true history of Death Valley have been told time and again in books and stories, in the movies and on television. The good guys and the bad guys, the swindlers and eccentrics. Walter Scott, known as Death Valley Scotty, was the most notorious character of them all, a flamboyant promoter who talked himself into international fame with tales of a gold mine that never existed. He befriended an eccentric insurance millionaire and used the man's money to build Scotty's Castle, the famous desert mansion that was fabulously appointed and never finished. Finally, Scott claimed all of Death Valley as his own. When the word reached him that the United States government had a national park in mind for the valley, he declared, "Why, doggone 'em, they're agoin' to make Death Valley—*my* Death Valley—into a so-and-so National Park for dudes." And they did just that (not just for dudes, but for other people as well).

Herbert Hoover, then president, signed the proclamation on February 11, 1933, creating Death Valley National Monument, which is about 2,900 square miles in area. It too was a lake once, as was the neighboring Panamint Valley. Overlooked by Telescope Peak, which is often capped with snow, Death Valley lies between the Panamint Range on the west and the Amargosa Range—the Black Mountains, the Funeral Mountains, and the Grapevine Mountains—on the east. The deepest part of the valley is near Badwater, 282 feet below sea level, the deepest land depression on the continent. Down in this valley a temperature of 134° F. in the shade was recorded in the summer of 1913, the hottest ever in the American desert (and almost as hot as any place on earth—only Azizia, Libya, in 1922, and San Luis Potosí, Mexico, in 1933, have been known to be hotter, both registering 136.4° F.).

The Panamint Indians, who were the inhabitants when the first white men arrived, called the place Tomesha, which in their Shoshonean dialect means "ground on fire," or "ground afire." (I was once in the valley in summer when the temperature was a mere unremarkable 125° F., and my strongest sensation was panic. Breathing was difficult, and the urge to try to claw myself out of the oppressive air was difficult to resist.)

In the winter, however, the valley's very nice, choice in fact, and very healthful—good and warm and dry in the daytime, cool to chilly at night. During this pleasant time of the year, visitors may camp out at any of the 12 campgrounds inside the monument, or they may stay at the rather posh Furnace Creek Inn, the cabins of the Furnace Creek Ranch, Scotty's Castle (which is now a museum with a few rooms to let by the Gospel Foundation), or in the cabins at the village of Stovepipe Wells.

The monument—formed by fire and cataclysm and the slowly violent rising, grinding, falling, and wearing away of the earth—is a mecca for geologists. With its strange formations and unearthly views; its crepe-hung mountains and deep, black craters; its white bats, prehistoric fish, and wild asses; its sudden cloudbursts; and its enormous boulders that move, apparently of their own accord, gouging trails behind them in the flats—the monument becomes one of the most sinister, most beautiful, most fascinating places in the coastal states.

Men went there in the early days for silver and gold, and they found some, as Panamint City, now a ghost town at the edge of the monument at the head of Surprise Canyon, and the ruins of Rhyolite, Ballarat, and Skidoo testify. The surprise was silver, discovered by a couple of outlaws laying low in the wilderness. For a few years Panamint City was the wildest, most murderous, most outrageous of all the outrageous towns of the West. Wells Fargo, a tough outfit, wouldn't touch it, and the only way the miners could get their silver out of the canyon without having it hijacked was to cast it into 500-pound balls: no bandit could sling one of *those* over his saddle and light out for the border. But silver petered out as the

silver market dropped. Then a monumental cloudburst sent thunderous floods through the canyon, washing away half the town and the road to the outside world. That was the end of Panamint City, except for the ghostly vestiges that remain for the vigorous traveler to explore.

But all the gold and silver that came out of the valley was small potatoes compared to the lodes in the Sierra foothills and in Nevada. The real treasure of Death Valley was borax, the "white gold" of the desert. Few people realize the vast commercial value of that mineral or its almost unlimited uses. It doesn't just clean grimy hands, it does that and it goes into detergents, but it also, in its various forms (the element boron is extracted from it), is used in glazing, in glassmaking—both window glass and the incredible space-age glasses that resist the sun's heat beyond the atmosphere—in welding and brazing and electroplating. It goes into alloys, synthetic fabrics, paper glazes, playing cards, antiseptics, cosmetics, plant food, flares, propellants, abrasives, nuclear-reactor control rods, flame-resistant paints, and many other products. For years the famous 20-mule teams took the borax out of the valley, but the discovery of much more accessible supplies in the Mojave Desert (at Boron, in Kern County, near Edwards Air Force Base) laid that enterprise to rest along with the silver and gold. The ruins of the borax works are there to see. So now, history, geology, scenery, climate, and a unique, natural world incorruptible are the treasures of Death Valley.

Eighty miles west and slightly north of Badwater, the deepest point, rises the loftiest, the highest mountain in the conterminous United States: Mt. Whitney, 14,495 feet. It's the crowning peak of the Sierra Nevada, but because of so many other peaks in that towering range, it hardly stands out at all. In fact, in 1871 Clarence King, the man who made the claim of being the first to scale it, went along happily for two years before it was pointed out to him that he had climbed the wrong mountain. He had climbed Mt. Langley, very nearby, instead.

These days, climbing Mt. Whitney is a popular long weekend's diversion, provided the ascent is made from the Owens Valley. There

the climber travels via a paved road from Lone Pine to the pack station at Whitney Portal (8,700 feet) and then by foot or horseback, through sagebrush and forests, into the High Country, crossing bare granite and ice and snow in his 13-mile trek to the top. Old folks and small children have climbed it, but it's scary sometimes along the narrow ledges of sheer precipice and razor-backed ridges. The trail is steep, and the air is thin indeed. Many climbers turn back, but well over 2,000 people every season reach the top and sign the register.

Mount Whitney and a dozen other peaks, nearly as high and thrown in together, along the eastern boundary of Sequoia and Kings Canyon national parks (contiguous preserves, Sequoia to the south, Kings Canyon to the north) are popularly called the High Sierra. This constitutes the southern end of the Sierra spine, which starts in a confused mixture with the Cascades in northeast California and pursues the California-Nevada border south through Lake Tahoe and on south to Yosemite. The mountains become more and more distinct and higher and higher—a wall between the Great Basin deserts of Nevada and the rich Central Valley. Then they continue south through Kings Canyon and Sequoia, taper down and curve seaward to become the lower range of the Tehachapis, and merge imperceptibly with the Coast Ranges north of Los Angeles.

Geologically the Sierra is a vast 400-mile slab of the earth's crust that has tilted upward like a trapdoor partially opened, leaving the western side a relatively smooth and gradual slant toward the floor of the valley and the eastern side a sheer, snowy, moisture-trapping escarpment of incredibly spectacular aspect when viewed from the deserts to the east. In the inconceivable pace and length of geological time, in those hundreds of millions of years that really can mean nothing to the minute-by-minute, day-by-day time-conception of the human mind—any more than can infinite space—three previous ranges of mountains, three Sierras, have risen up and been worn away by the everyday forces of nature. The present Sierras take their shapes from the tilting and

buckling of the earth's crust; the rising up of molten rock through the faults and crevices; volcanic action; and the slow, inexorable, grinding movement of ice during the age of Pleistocene glaciers.

The monumental architecture of the Yosemite Valley, the heart of Yosemite National Park and perhaps the most beautiful valley on the face of the earth (with the possible exception of the fabled Vale of Kashmir, which I have never seen), was carved largely by the movement of ice. North Dome, Half Dome, El Capitán, Cathedral Spires, Sentinel Dome, Sentinel Rock—great slabs of sheer granite thousands of feet high—rise on either side of the Yosemite Valley, which is the valley of the Merced River. Into the river plunge the cold crystal-clear waterfalls for which this area is so famous.

Yosemite's not a large valley, no more than a few miles long and narrow even at its widest point. It's the ideal mountain valley—with its flat, green floor; its cottonwoods, oaks, and maples that turn to red and gold in autumn; its quiet dark green firs and pines; and its rock-strewn pure tumbling river. It's also, unfortunately, so crowded in summer that you can't see the valley for the people—ten, twenty, thirty thousand at a time—and all the equipment they bring. Again, as in the clear desert, smog has become a condition of life in recent summers in the high, pure air of the purest of mountains. In 1970 the overcrowding and exhaust pollution became so acute that many of the roads were closed to automobile traffic, and open-air shuttle buses were run from peripheral parking lots into the valley.

Yet the valley is only one small part of the nearly 1,200 square miles of the national park. The High Country north of the Tioga Pass Road is interlaced with hiking trails and campsites, with woods, meadows, peaks, and canyons and thousands of lakes and streams whose sweet waters are full of fish. And there is no smog in the High Country. The High Country is accessible by road in summer, the Tioga Road, the only road through the park connecting east and west by way of Tioga Pass (9,941 feet), a pass that, even after the extensive alterations (widening and so forth here and there) made

in recent years, must remain one of the most hair-raisingly exciting automobile passes in the western states. The views are indescribable, but nervous drivers or drivers with nervous passengers should not essay it. The pass and the road are seldom open before the middle of June and they usually close on October 1.

Yosemite Valley is open all year round, and after the summer crowds have come and gone, a golden halcyon peace descends—the trees change color, the nights grow nippy, and cheery blazes in the cabins' fireplaces are needed and welcome. Then the snows come, and the creeks and the waterfalls freeze. The people who have made their reservations way back in the summer come to spend their Christmases in Yosemite View Lodge or the Ahwahnee Hotel. Christmas is a lovely time in the valley of the River of Our Lady of Mercy.

The Merced River rises in a dozen lakes and streams of the High Country southeast of the valley where the park comes together with the Sierra National Forest. In this high region too the streams begin to gather to make the San Joaquin River, which together with the Sacramento, waters the great Central Valley and eventually empties into the Pacific through San Francisco Bay.

On the narrow, roaring Middle Fork of this nascent waterway, the Devils Postpile National Monument (not far outside the confines of Yosemite but accessible by road only from the east) displays those bizarre prismlike columns of basaltic rock, formed by volcanism and eroded by ice, that are found many places in the world, such as Fingal's Cave, in Scotland, and the Giant's Causeway, in Ireland. Here in the monument, the columns are nearly vertical and from 40 to 60 feet tall. That strange stuff, pumice, the "rock that floats" and the companion to lava, is found here too. There is also a fine waterfall, Rainbow Falls, where the San Joaquin makes a straight drop of 140 feet into a rainbow-haloed pool. On the road to the monument are the Mammoth Lakes, a fishing and skiing area now, but once the site of Mammoth City, one of the shortest-lived gold-mining towns in the state. In 1878 it had a population of 125, and by the next year there were 2,500 people, but the winter of that year,

1879-80, was so harsh and severe that almost everyone abandoned the gold and left, and those who didn't froze to death.

The Devils Postpile National Monument is a way station on the John Muir Trail between Yosemite and Kings Canyon-Sequoia national parks. John Muir, of course, was the famous naturalist, geologist, mountaineer, author, and forceful champion of national parks. He was one of the founders of the Sierra Club and an explorer of the West and Alaska, and in fact, much of the world. A major trail in the High Sierra was dedicated to him after he died in 1914, and dozens of places from California to Alaska bear his name.

Though there are "Big Trees" in Yosemite, the biggest and the most numerous are in the transitional forests of Sequoia and Kings Canyon national parks. Along the Generals Highway in the lower and western section of the parks, the *Sequoia gigantea* appear singly and in groves among the firs, pines, and cedars. Had the scribes or whoever it was that determined the wonders of the ancient world had access to this Pacific Coast and had seen these trees (though those now standing would have probably been mere adolescents then, there would have been other grown-up trees for the judges to wonder at), they surely would have put them on their list. Even cinematography fails to convey the immanent reality of these trees, which cannot be apprehended just with the movement of the eye from forest floor to sky, by walking around or even, in some cases, through the massive trunks, or by measurements or statistics. In order to believe them, one must feel their living *presence*.

I left my cabin at Pinewood Camp in Giant Forest (where the lodge, the grocery store, the coffee shop, the ranger station, the post office, and so forth are) and walked the trails through the groves about six o'clock one morning. The forest was still misty and wet with dew, the mosquitoes had not yet arisen, and any wild creatures that were up and about were foraging in the sunny meadows on the other side of the ridge. As I walked, climbing slightly, I moved through the steadily dissipating mist, passing among the gigantic trunks as if I were passing silently among the columns of the Great Temple of Ammon at Karnak. Yet these mammoth trees were alive, and I felt they knew that I was there. After all, *they* had been there for thousands of years, and their ancestors for millions. They were dominant members of that steamy, luxuriant, fernlike, cycadaceous, weirdly fingered forest community that covered most of the Northern Hemisphere before the ice came.

After the ice left, only those trees in the Sierras remained on earth, and they still grow —young ones and middle-aged ones and, I would say, old ones, except that the oldest tree in the Giant Forest is less than 4,000 years old. Barring the greedy or capricious hand of man or a cataclysm of nature, the tree should have hundreds of years to go before it dies of old age. Attempts have been made to raise these beings from another age, from an earlier earth, elsewhere in the modern world, but they either decline to grow altogether, as in the Atlantic states, or do poorly, as in England, where, according to one British horticulturist, they can be planted "only as an ornament of the lawn or paddock."

The largest tree, indeed the largest living thing on earth by sheer mass, is the General Sherman Tree just off the Generals Highway. It is 272 feet 4 inches tall and its base, which looks like the foot of a great red elephant, is 101 feet 7 inches around. If it were cut up into one-by-tens and two-by-fours as many a lumberman, with alacrity, would do, it would build about 45 three-bedroom houses—all from a seed the size of a pinhead and weighing 1/6000th of an ounce.

The General Sherman Tree was first named the Karl Marx Tree, in 1886, by the Kaweah

Co-operative Commonwealth Colony, a socialistic utopian society which planned to cut timber in the area, but which officially vowed never to cut the Big Trees. Nevertheless, the established lumbermen—who had been slaughtering the Big Trees wholesale—became alarmed, as did the United States Government. After much talk and squabbling and litigation, the Giant Forest was proclaimed a national park (Sequoia) in 1890, the second (the first was Yellowstone) national park in the nation (Yosemite became a park the same year). Later Sequoia was greatly enlarged, and the adjoining Kings Canyon was designated a national park in 1940.

Although nearly 2 million people visit the parks each year, most of them stick to the highways through the easily accessible Big Trees groves or through Kings Canyon itself, ignoring the hundreds of miles of gorgeous wild country, the wildest of all the Sierra, that make up most of the preserve. Interlaced with hiking and horseback trails, the High Country is a vast, friendly, unbroken wilderness of lakes and rivers and meadows and mountains and canyons and, in the winter, snow.

The great Sierra snowpack, created by the saturated storms from the Pacific Ocean (they roll in like fat, dripping water bags and are punctured by the high, cold mountain peaks), stretches from the Tehachapis north through the High Sierra, Lake Tahoe, Lassen Peak, and Mt. Shasta, where the Sierras become confused with the Cascades. The pack deepens from November to April, and when the season changes and the spring sun comes out to stay, the runoff of melting snow pours over the massive granite of the mountains and down the canyons through thousands of branches and forks of hundreds of streams, making dozens of rivers—the Pit, the Sacramento, the Deer, the Rock, the Butte, the Feather, the Yuba, the Bear, the American, the Rubicon, the Cosumnes, the Mokelumne, the Stanislaus, the Tuolumne, the Merced, the Fresno, the San Joaquin, the Kings, the Tule, the Kaweah, and the Kern—to name a few.

Before the snow melts, however, hundreds of thousands of people bundle up, put antifreeze in their radiators, chains in their trunks,

spirits and hot liquids in their Thermoses, and head for the high hills from the San Bernardino Mountains outside Los Angeles to Mt. Shasta near the Oregon line. It's the ski migration, a weekend flow and ebb from coast and valley to mountain and back. Lake Tahoe, an enormously popular summer resort (now severely threatened by pollution), lies in the area of the heaviest snow which falls on the peaks and in the valleys to the west. Mark Twain called this lake "a noble sheet of blue water" and he wrote: ". . . walled in by a rim of snow-clad peaks . . . it lay there with the shadows of the mountains brilliantly photographed upon its still surface, [and] I thought it must surely be the fairest picture the whole earth affords. . . ."

This is not an area of extreme sustained cold. In fact, Squaw Valley, in preparing for the winter Olympics of 1960 found that the ice rinks had to be artificially refrigerated to keep them frozen. But the snow! It was the snow that trapped the Donner Party in the winter of 1846. In late October, the snow, which had come early that year, as it sometimes does, blocked the pass, driving the game to lower elevations and compelling the emigrants in their shelters of brush and branches to eat the hides of their dead, worn-out animals, the rawhide from their boots, and finally, each other. Now, of course, Donner Lake offers swimming and water sports in the summer and skating and sledding in winter, and Donner Peak and Emigrant Gap are surrounded by lodges, rope and chair lifts, cabins, stores, bars, and cafés; but people still get snowbound.

North of Lake Tahoe the Sierra Nevadas angle westward toward the center of the state and soon become intermingled, confused, and finally integrated with the Cascade Range that carries on northwestward all the way to Canada. Lassen Peak, in Lassen Volcanic National Park, is the only active volcano in the Pacific Coast states. Its last sequence of eruptions began in 1914 and went on for seven years, during which time the mountain blew off devastating steam, smoke, ash, and lava. It's quiet now, and volcanologists say it's dying. At any rate, Lassen park and the Lava Beds National Monument farther

north are the best places in the United States, aside from distant fiery Hawaii, to view volcanic activity recent and ancient.

The lava beds are very old and contain cinder cones and lava flows that issued from fissures in the earth, rolling out like black porridge and forming caves and tunnels and "tubes" and "chimneys," which became the sheltered hideouts for the Modoc Indians, led by their chief, Captain Jack, during their last stand against the white invaders. South of the monument stands a mountain nearly 8,000 feet high made of black obsidian, a mountain of glass. All is old and quiet at the lava beds, but Lassen Peak is surrounded by constantly bubbling, boiling pots of red mud, perilously hot. Steam hisses from the rocks, and there's a persistent smell of brimstone in the air. Within the park too are more than 50 quiet lakes that draw deer and bear to their clear, trout-filled waters and mirror the many mountain peaks as well as the snow-covered volcano itself. Because of the winter snows, Lassen is mostly a summer park, though a small corner in the southwest is kept open for skiing.

In the same Cascade chain to the northwest of Lassen Peak is Mt. Shasta, described by Joaquin Miller as "Lonely as God and white as a winter moon, [it] starts up sudden and solitary from the heart of the great black forest." Indeed, it dominates the countryside for a hundred miles. It is, as John Muir says, ". . . a fire mountain, an old volcano . . . , " with its sides gouged by ice and its upper reaches still alive with glaciers. Its lower elevations are heavily populated with villages, motels, hotels, and lodges, for it's the focus of a large and popular recreation area, with skiing in winter and general vacationing in summer. It's an easy mountain to climb; in fact, it's been ascended in less than 2½ hours. Like the Yosemite Valley and Lake Tahoe, it has been heavily commercialized.

All those rivers from all that snow feed the reservoirs and the 20,000 miles of irrigation waterworks (canals, sloughs, aqueducts, ditches and pipes) of the great Central Valley, a rich alluvial plain nearly as big and generally the same shape as Lake Michigan, and itself once a freshwater lake in preglacial times.

Completely surrounded by mountains, the valley—flat, tedious, interminable, dusty and torrid in summer, subject to killer tule fogs in winter—is the nation's most prodigious agricultural machine. It is the major production area of a state that grows fully a third of the country's fruits and vegetables, more cotton than any other state except Texas, and the sole producer of many "specialty" crops. The list of its products is endless; rice, sugar beets, most vegetables, grapes and raisins, most noncitrus fruits, almonds and walnuts, olives, well, as I said, the list goes on and on.

The Central Valley can be pretty in the spring when the fruit trees are in blossom and the wild mustard blooms between the orchard rows, but once the quick blush of April fades, a pall—of dust and heavy labor, fertilizer and serious business, and in some places, a greasy petroleum smell—hangs over all creation as far as you can see. The towns lined up along Highway 99, which runs through the center of the valley like a spinal cord, can scarcely be distinguished one from the other, being repetitive aggregations of used-car lots, gas stations, and truck stops. Drab or not, the wealth is there in the irrigated earth, and the huge agricultural corporations that mine the wealth of this tedium are very rich indeed.

Of these towns, Sacramento, of course, is an exception. (In the old days, John Sutter's famous fort and boat landing, which was the end of the emigrant trail, stood on the same site.) The 1970 census gives Sacramento 254,413 people, with over 1½ times that many more in the metropolitan area, so it's considerably more than a town. The city itself added about 63,000 people in the ten years between censuses. Many people, however, particularly those more accustomed to the sophistication of San Francisco or the glittering chaos of Los Angeles, who are compelled to reside in Sacramento because of government business or assignment complain of its being, regardless of its size, a small town. At the same time, many old residents look upon its sprawling thousands and its fearsome noise and traffic with dismay. "If it gets any worse we'll all have to head for the hills," one resident said. There are still many quiet, shady streets, lined with tall trees and two-story houses with scroll-saw-work on the outside and occupants within who still use "Sacto" as the return address on their letters and eschew ZIP codes. Nevertheless, the city is the capital and seat of government of the most populous state in the Union. It has two airports, two Air Force bases, an army supply depot, three colleges, two large aerospace industries, and a deep-sea port to which oceangoing vessels from the world around ply their way up the river, through the delta marshes, and along the ship channel to the seaport in the middle of the great Central Valley. It'll never be Sutter's Landing again.

The mountains that wall in the valley on the west are the Coast Ranges: new mountains, mountains still forming though not so swiftly that you would notice. The Coast Range diastrophism, as the geologists call it, began probably in the late Pliocene period, or about 5 million years ago. From south to north they begin in southern California and end up in southern Alaska. Compared to the Sierras, the Coast Ranges are not very big mountains, though some of the peaks in the south exceed 10,000 feet. In general they run north and south in parallel ranges, sometimes with sizable valleys between. In the south, though, the Santa Ynez, the San Gabriel, the Santa Monica, the Santa Susana, and the San Bernardino mountains—the Transverse Ranges—run crosswise. In the north of California near Oregon, the Trinity, the Marble, the Salmon, and the Siskiyou are jumbled in every direction, mixing in with the Cascades. While not lofty, some of the Coast Ranges are as rugged and steep as the Andes. They often rise straight from the sea and back into the interior with one precipitous forested canyon after another. Some of the ranges—treeless and grass-covered—stretch out sensuously rounded and curved, like houris or odalisques or tawny pumas languidly taking the summer sun.

In the wilder ranges, such as the San Rafael and the Santa Lucia mountains, in nearly inaccessible wilderness, most of the original creatures of nature remain—except the California grizzly which was exterminated early in the state's history. In the Sespe Condor Sanctuary, northwest of Los Angeles near the newly designated San Rafael Wilderness, the few remaining California condors reside. They, along with the Andean condor—now also a very rare bird—with a ten-foot wingspan, are the largest land birds in the Western Hemisphere. In these rugged ranges, deer, of course, and all the smaller mammals are plentiful: foxes, squirrels, rabbits, raccoon, and so forth, and some bears. There are wild boars and wild turkeys and a great diversity of smaller birds, including the funny topknot California quails, the soft gray, ubiquitous doves, and the water ouzels. Bobcats (the native lynx) are found here, and sometimes a rare mountain lion. One springtime I saw a lion cub far up a fragrant canyon in the Santa Lucias drinking, unaware of my eyes upon it, from a cold rushing stream. The sunlight glanced off its young golden fur. Except for the running of water over stones, the canyon was silent as a cloud. It was a rare and pleasant sight.

Fragrance, the smell of brush and flowers fresh from the winter rains, is one of the amenities of spring in the Coast Ranges. Sweet broom, lupine, and wild lilac mix with the dusty mothlike scent of sage and manzanita. At the Pinnacles National Monument, in the Gabilan Range east of the Salinas Valley, the predominant springtime smell is wild lilac, or buckbrush, a tall, bushy shrub with millions of tiny blossoms, pale lavender to deep violet blue. It forms a vital part of the plant community of the monument, the chaparral, which is a combination of manzanita, chamisa, holly-leaved cherry, and other shrubby plants that grow closely together, requiring little water and holding the sparse soil to the steep hillsides. The chaparral, scratchy and persistent, grows as dense and impenetrable as any Corsican maquis. (The leather chaps that cowboys wear to protect their legs from the heavy brush derive their name from chaparral.) The Pinnacles monument was, 30 million years ago, a volcano that blew up, and 30 million years of rain, wind, sun, and frost have left only great towers of rock and gargantuan boulders tossed on top of each other, forming caves and tunnels and dark, wet passageways where Moses Spring runs through. Little known and infrequently visited, the monument is a wondrous place for campers and kids when the flowers bloom and the grass is green, but it's dry and hot as hell in summer.

In the thousand or so miles of mountainous California coast from Mexico to Oregon, only two natural breaches in the rocky shore—San Francisco Bay and San Diego—offer safe harbor for the large vessels of the sea. Juan Rodriguez Cabrillo, a Portuguese navigator in the employ of the Spanish governor of Guatemala, was the first European to set foot in California. He went ashore at San Diego and, as was the custom of the time, claimed all the land for the king of Spain, neglecting to ask the permission of the Indians who already lived there. That was in 1542. Nearly 300 years later, Richard Henry Dana, of Cambridge, a Harvard dropout turned seaman, described San Diego as he saw it: "The Harbor is small and landlocked; there is no surf; the vessels lie within a cable's length of the beach, and the beach itself is smooth hard sand without rocks or stones." Cabrillo called it a "closed and very good port," and there is a statue of him, long hair and beard, sword, cape, and cross of Spain, gazing out from the modest height of the point over the long, blue bay. (Dana apparently, and possibly Cabrillo too, saw only the north bay, missing the huge extension that curves south for miles past Coronado Peninsula.) Cabrillo's statue and the old Point Loma lighthouse are part of a national monument. In the monument too a whale-watching station offers a good view of the annual migration of the California gray whales on their way to Scammon's Lagoon and other breeding grounds in Baja California. A statue, a lighthouse, and a view of the sea don't sound like much, but more people visit Cabrillo National Monument than any other national monument, including the Statue of Liberty in New York Harbor.

San Diego is oriented—if such a term may be used for a city looking west—to the sea. Its large, secure harbor, from old Spanish times until today, has been the home of fishermen, shipping concerns, and the navy. The navy is still the biggest industry, and a brief citing of naval installations will show why. The city is headquarters for the Eleventh Naval District.

There are also a naval supply depot, a naval hospital, a naval sonar school, a naval radio station, a naval electronics laboratory, a naval air station on North Island, a naval air station at Miramar, a naval amphibious base, and a naval training center. The Marine Corps also has a recruit training center there, and there's a Coast Guard air base. The city is also the center of the huge aerospace industry. Four colleges and universities have campuses in the San Diego vicinity, as do five junior colleges. The city has gained more than 123,000 people since 1960, attaining a population in 1970 of 696,769 and making it only slightly less populated than San Francisco.

Though it's generally considered to be a conservative city, an easygoing ambiance prevails, partly because of its traditional Spanish past and its large Spanish-American population, and partly because of its climate, which is really as fine as its civic boosters say. It's warm most of the time, seldom very hot, a city of sunshine and flowers and pleasant breezes from the sea. It may be the only major city in the world whose international airport is only ten minutes from downtown. La Jolla ("the jewel"), northwest of San Diego, is a kind of oceanside Palm Springs—very posh, very pretty, very expensive. Wonderful rocks and surf and clear blue water. A jewel if you can afford it.

Oddly enough, San Pedro Bay, the seaport handling the most tonnage and the most passengers on the West Coast, emerged from a very unpromising location indeed. Dana had disparaging words to say about this bay: "What brought us into such a place, we could not conceive . . . for we lay exposed to every wind that could blow, except the northerly winds, and they came over a flat country with a rake of more than a league of water." In spite of its shallowness and exposure, the bay has been made the entrance to an almost wholly man-made seaport, the Port of Los Angeles.

Los Angeles itself, if such a place can be said to exist, is not one city, or in fact, any city—it's a vicinity. It includes Santa Catalina Island, 27 miles out into the Pacific Ocean. It also includes the port and the San Fernando Valley, miles from each other, and in between are dozens of towns and cities, such as Santa Monica, Beverly Hills, Pasadena, Long Beach, and in the Mojave Desert, Lancaster and Palmdale, and many others—all part of Los Angeles County. Somewhere within that vicinity *is* a City of Los Angeles with 2,816,061 people (preliminary 1970 census), the third largest city in the nation, but if all those cities within the county are counted in, the population rises to a staggering 8 million-plus, almost all of whom drive cars.

Smog, of course, is a national fact of life, but of all the places in America in which a prototypical culture exemplified by southern California should *not* have been developed, it is in the Los Angeles basin, where the proximity to the cool sea, the heavy sunshine, the enclosing hills and mountains make it the perfect temperature-inversion photochemical trap. If you can manage to breathe there, however, many places and things may be enjoyed. There's money to be made, if that's your pleasure, and there's a great variety of ethnic and social cultures to observe. It's not all glamour and high-rise: there are many quiet, shady streets, with bungalows and neat, pleasant houses right in the middle of Hollywood. The freeway system, particularly downtown at "the Stack"—where the Hollywood, the Harbor, the Santa Ana, and the Pasadena freeways converge—stands as the crowning achievement of the surrealistic imagination of technological man. Money may be spent too, if that's your pleasure. Good living is to be had at every turn. The new music center, the new county art museum, new theaters, new hotels, new auditoriums, and new arenas provide pleasure, entertainment, and accommodations of various types and levels, all first-rate of their kinds. There are many industries, mostly of light, specialized varieties—movies, broadcasting, recording, television—and electronics, aerospace, oil, and real estate. The colleges and universities—Occidental College, University of California at Los Angeles, California State College, University of Southern California, California Institute of the Arts—educate hundreds of thousands of young people who, when school is out, throng to the miles and miles of beaches, mostly along Santa Monica Bay, where the summer-long rituals of sun, sex, and surf take place.

The southern beaches extend with some, but not many, breaks as far as Santa Barbara, that city singularly blessed with the climate and luxuriance of Eden itself. The Santa Ynez Mountains behind the city provide plenty of water, Point Conception breaks all but the most determined winter winds, the sun shines generously, and the countryside around blooms and burgeons with the flowers and scents of orange and lemon trees.

Offshore lie the northern members of the Santa Barbara Islands, or Channel Islands, some of which were proclaimed a national monument in 1938. These islands have sheer cliffs, caves, and sea-cut arches. No one lives there except a park ranger in summer. They are heavily populated, however, by cormorants, pelicans, and many other sea birds, and by sea lions, sea elephants, the rare sea otter, and the even rarer Guadalupe fur seal. In spring the islands burst forth in blossom. Being so isolated over the many centuries, they have developed unique species of trees, shrubs, and ground plants.

North of Santa Barbara, above the ocean, is La Cuesta Encantada ("the enchanted hill").

Here, William Randolph Hearst, the eccentric publisher, assembled his vast pleasure dome, La Casa Grande, ransacking Europe and the Mediterranean for sculpture, hangings, parts of monasteries, Pompeian tiles, Roman columns, and Spanish palatial facades. It was never finished, and a great deal of what he bought is still in storage. La Casa Grande is part of the Hearst San Simeon State Historical Monument now, and thousands of people visit it each year. It has created, by going public, a brand-new tourist industry and motel trade on what used to be a pastoral, lonesome edge of the Pacific.

From San Simeon north to Carmel, the coast, where the Santa Lucias rise straight from the sea, is very rugged and very grand. When the summer fogs cover the cliffs and the foghorns wail, the sea lions bark below on the rocks, and the gulls, hidden in mist, squawk like disembodied spirits, it can be spooky; and in winter, taking full-face the brunt of the violent storms, it can also be dangerous, for the road may wash out at some place or the cliffs slide or boulders fall.

Carmel (called Carmel-by-the-Sea to avoid confusion with another Carmel that once stood a few miles away) evolved from a group of cabins and woodsy shacks erected in the early years of this century by some artists and writers escaping from the tumult of the city. Those early residents battled "progress" and won a few small points (there are no house numbers, no mail delivery, and some of the streets aren't paved), but they lost on the big point, freedom from tumult. Though the town's permanent population has remained roughly the same over the last two decades, the visiting population, particularly on holidays and weekends, creates a tumultuous scene. Automobiles glut the quaint streets, and people swarm over the sidewalks visiting the myriad little expensive shoppes and, with luck, making their way to the beach which, regardless of the suffocating character of the town, remains one of the most beautiful in the state. The water is a good Mediterranean indigo blue, the sand is white, and the surf crashes dramatically upon the rocks at either end of Carmel Bay.

The wooded, residential areas in the north part of town lead into, by way of a toll gate, Pebble Beach and the Del Monte estates, an exclusive Monterey Peninsula residential and recreation area circumscribed by the Seventeen Mile Drive, a toll road that winds along the cliffs and past the ancient rocks and ancient twisted cypresses growing above the crashing dark blue water. Only in this region do the Monterey cypresses grow natively, though they have been planted successfully elsewhere. They lend enormous character to an otherwise exposed and rather featureless piece of real estate. That very featurelessness, however, provides excellent ground for the sports that rich people do seem traditionally to enjoy: riding, polo, and golf. There are stables, at least one polo field, and five golf courses within the confines of the estates, and in the middle of one course is a deserted Indian village.

Long before the first escapees from the city put up their retreats in Carmel and long before the Pacific Improvement Company began to construct its elegant playgrounds on the Monterey Peninsula, Miguel José Serra, called Junipero, a Franciscan brother (and as celebrated a name in California history as Frémont or Sutter), landed in Monterey Bay (1770). He founded a mission there and moved it the next year to a site near the mouth of the Carmel River, where it, or part of it, still stands, bathed in sunshine—its scaly old walls quick with lizards, and its gardens and graveyard lush with flowers. The energetic Serra, who had established San Diego de Alcalá earlier, and who was to create a chain of missions up and down the edge of California, considered Misión San Carlos Borromeo del Río Carmelo his home, and he is buried there. Other missions, some begun by Serra and some by others, still stand in places in the state. Some of them are in virtual ruins, others have been restored or rebuilt so completely as to be unrecognizable as anything but modern churches (San Rafael, San Luis Obispo). Some have been partially restored to display what they were once possibly like (Santa Ynez, San Antonio de Padua, San Francisco de Solano), while others still display much of the original structure in various states of repair (San Juan Capistrano, San Juan Bautista).

In 1776 Father Serra founded the Misión San Francisco de Asis, and though the city that eventually grew up in the hills and sand dunes near the mission took its name from St. Francis, the mission itself came to be popularly known as Mission Dolores because of marshland in the vicinity called Laguna de Nuestra Señora de los Dolores ("Lagoon of our Lady of the Sorrows"), and so it is known today. It survived the 1906 earthquake and seems destined to survive the heavy rumbling of traffic along Dolores Street in San Francisco's mission district.

San Francisco, or simply "The City" in popular reference, occupies the tip end of a peninsula separating San Francisco Bay, or simply "The Bay," from the Pacific Ocean. The city (and the corresponding county of San Francisco) is rigidly confined geographically and thus, unlike Los Angeles, which is constantly spilling over into unincorporated areas, cannot be expanded. Though the entire area surrounding the bay grows apace, the city itself loses people, or rather, residents, who spread out more and more into suburbia and come into the city to work. According to preliminary 1970 figures the city lost 25,000 residents in the last ten years. It's still the center and the heart of a vast area of north-central California; all roads and bridges (and, in the near future, subways) lead to the city, whose international airport handles the fourth largest volume of traffic in the country.

No one, I think, except perhaps some dedicated provincials from Omaha or Atlanta, would deny that San Francisco is the most beautiful city in America, possibly the world, though it would probably take a dedicated provincial from San Francisco to make the latter claim. The magical summer fog, the hills, the sunsets, the blue water, the Golden Gate Bridge, the great green park, the miles and miles of ocean beach, the enchanted winter light on rows of white houses and towering walls of glass—all these and many other amenities that the city affords have been photographed, written about, sung about, poeticized about with perfect legitimacy.

San Francisco has, of course, all the problems of major cities everywhere—overcrowd-ing (despite its dropping population), crime, air and water pollution, taxes, garbage—and with police, schools, and races, as well as a few unique problems of its own. But it has also been and continues to be the spawning ground for many an emergent popular culture—artistic, literary, musical—as well as a solid base for such established forms of high-style entertainment as opera, symphony, art, and theater. It's a small town too. It's almost impossible to pass by Union Square or cross the intersection of Grant and Post or even walk through Woolworth's or stroll under the trimmed sycamores of Golden Gate Park on Sunday afternoon, while the band in the park blares out "Over the Waves," without running into someone you know.

It may also be the only city in the whole world these days that within 20 minutes by car you can be out of and wandering or hiking or driving through open country, over untenanted hills and mountains, and through deep forests.

Muir Woods National Monument, almost 500 acres of giant coast redwoods, is only 17 miles from the city. Another 17 miles farther north is Point Reyes National Seashore, a relatively undeveloped area of rocks and tableland, white cliffs and long, long, curving beaches with perilous surf, crags and forested ridges, hiking and riding trails, quiet lagoons and oyster beds, dairy farms, wind, and wild flowers, driftwood, sand dunes, and deer. The notorious San Andreas Fault, the prodigious crack in the earth's crust that caused San Francisco to shake so in 1906 (and again, less violently, in 1957), can best be observed in this region, from Bolinas Lagoon through the Olema Valley and along Tomales Bay. Farther north, the coast again becomes extremely precipitous in the vincinity of Fort Ross, where in the early nineteenth century, the Russians maintained a village, a farm, and a boat harbor devoted to the capture of the highly prized sea otter and fur seal. The restored chapel of Fort Ross, a state historical monument, was mysteriously destroyed by fire in the hot, dry autumn of 1970.

The north coast is almost exclusively devoted to lumber as an industry and to forests as a natural feature. This is a land of giant redwoods *(Sequoia sempervirens),* related to

the Big Trees of the Sierra, though not as old or as big around, but taller.

In the new Redwoods National Park—it was designated a national park in 1968—the tallest of the trees yet discovered and measured is 367.8 feet, more than twice as tall as the Statue of Liberty. "John Muir called these forests churches," I wrote elsewhere a few years ago (so I'm quoting myself now), "which of course is sentimental Holy Grailery and Wagnerian Romanticism, but the trees do stand as high as some cathedrals, sunlight does fall through in slanted beams as through the clerestory windows of Mainz or Worms, and the sea breeze caught in the treetops could be construed as a Heavenly Choir. Whatever each individual might feel—beatitude, peace, awe, wonder—the redwood forest is a cool instinctual jungle that touches something very deep in the primitive human psyche. In the spring these forests' floors blossom with rhododendron and wild azalea. Man-sized ferns grow along the creeks. Orchids and violets thrive in the mossy places. The carpet of soft needles makes anyplace you care to lie a bed, and nearly every wild creature of the woods lives there."

Redwoods love water. They live along creeks and up wet, coastal canyons, and along the beaches where the rivers join the sea. They are nourished particularly by the heavy, daily summer fogs of the north coast. The green wood is so heavy it sinks in a mill pond, and the living trees resist fire, insects, and disease. That's why they live so long. They do not, of course, resist the faller's chain saw. As a youth I worked as a bucker and choker-setter for an outfit out of Sacramento called Lumbermen's Supply. When I think how close we came to cutting the very groves, the very individual trees, that have now, finally, been brought under protection, I quake a little.

Rain is as much a fact of life on the north coast as lack of it is in the desert; but for all the rain that falls in that part of California, it's nothing to the wetness of the coasts of the great Northwest.

Near San Diego Bay and Los Guijarros (Ballast Point) at the tip of Point Loma headland, shown here, Spanish explorers, led by Adm. Juan Rodriguez Cabrillo, a Portuguese, for the first time sighted in 1542 the American west coast. On the horizon, Mexico.

Within the great seaport city of San Diego are 17½ miles of Pacific shoreline; within the county 30,000 pleasure boats are registered. The center of San Diego—with its bay and zoo and Balboa Park and impressive skyline—is a good jumping-off place for La Jolla, Scripps aquarium and museum, Seal Rock, Misión San Diego de Alcalá, Torrey Pines, or the Anza-Borrego Desert, Salton Sea, and Mexico.

Misión San Juan Capistrano in southern California was founded in 1776 by Father Junipero Serra, whose statue is in the background. Although swallows return annually to the mission on St. Joseph's Day (March 19), the white pigeons appear hourly at the fountain.

One feature of Joshua Tree National Monument is the many square miles of quartz monzonite rock that thrust high above the desert floor. Many varieties of cactus and other plant life thrive in the 1,000 to 6,000 foot elevation of this very dry land in southern California.

The Mojave Desert, an arid basin with sparse vegetation and a remarkably hostile environment.

Upper left: Seen here are the innumerable lights of Hollywood and the many communities in the vast Los Angeles lowlands. Not seen, however, are La Brea Tar Pits, County Art Museum, Harbor Freeway, or Hollywood and Vine.

Lower left: Avalon is the principal port and population and resort center of 25-mile-long Santa Catalina Island, which is 27 miles from Los Angeles Harbor. Most of the island is ruggedly wild and uninhabited, although some farms and ranches are in the valleys.

Right: San Simeon, William Randolph Hearst's estate, has been since 1958 a state historical monument. It is located on a high knoll of the Santa Lucia mountains.

The flower above is scarlet gilia, a trumpet flower.

Sprinkler irrigation sprays the lettuce, spinach, artichokes, and various other crops of the 10-by-40-mile immensely fertile Salinas Valley. Cattle range on each side of the valley. To the west are the Santa Lucia mountains; to the east is the Gabilan Range.

On preceding page: Point Lobos Reserve is a rockbound, 1,250-acre peninsula below Carmel Highlands and is noted for a protected grove of Monterey cypress. A scenic road is augmented by picnic areas and a network of nature trails with access to coves and beach areas, where sea lions and sea otters can be seen on offshore rocks and in kelp beds. No plant or rock may be removed from the park.

Reflected in the irrigation canal of Owens Valley are the autumn-tinted cottonwoods and blue shadows of the Sierra Nevada's eastern slopes. The valley's elevation is 4,000 feet.

Left: The Founders Group is one of several groves of giant sequoias that can be visited on the Congress Trail in Sequoia National Park. The trees grow only on the western slope of the Sierras at elevations of 4,000 to 8,000 feet.

Towering over Death Valley National Monument are the Funeral Mountains
of the Amargosa Range. The view is from Zabriskie Point. The time, day's end.

The flower, a wild currant.

This 200-foot-wide California aqueduct carries water from the Sacramento and
San Joaquin delta for about 200 miles along the western edge of Central Valley.
The water is stored in reservoirs like the San Luis. In the background is the Delta Mendota Canal.

Here the Tuolumne River leaves Tuolumne Meadows in Yosemite National Park. This parkland area, which is crossed by the high Tioga Pass Road, is the largest meadow in California's Sierras.

Upper left: San Francisco is like no other city in the world. It is fascinating and delightful, and its skyline and Bay bridge are shown here at twilight. Marshall Saunders, years ago, said, "San Francisco is not the back door of the continent. San Francisco is the front door." It is.

Lower left: Half Dome, towering nearly 5,000 feet above the Merced River, is the most conspicuous, unique, and well-known rock formation in Yosemite National Park. On the back, or dome, side of the mountain are steps cut in the granite and cables to aid climbers. Experts have also scaled the vertical face, but not easily.

Above: The source of the narrow waterfalls tumbling down these slopes is Shadow Lake. The location is Minaret Wilderness in the High Sierras.

The Minarets are in the heart of California's Minaret Wilderness, a spectacular area.

Opposite page: El Capitán is a sheer rock monolith that rises 3,580 feet above the Merced River in Yosemite. This picture was taken on a frosty October morning. Yosemite Valley is seven miles long and about a mile in width. The national park encompasses 1,189 square miles of the Sierra Nevadas, with elevations from 2,000 to 12,000 feet.

Wild rose

Foxtail barley

Star tulip

An early morning fog fills the lowlands just south of Lake Crowley at the upper end of Owens Valley. Clouds are crossing the distant White Mountains.

Unusually shaped mineral deposits called tufa towers line the shore of Mono Lake
in the eastern foothills of the Sierra Nevadas. Mono, elevation 6,400 feet, is all that
remains of a larger and deeper Ice-Age lake, Lake Russell. The Sierras and
US 395 are on the west side, Mono Craters on the south.

Opposite page: In a canyon quarried by glacial action, basalt columns 60 feet high
stand above those fallen from the lava face of Devils Postpile National Monument.
The monument, 900 feet long and 200 feet high, is situated at a 7,600-foot elevation
on the Middle Fork of the San Joaquin River in California's Sierras.

This view of the Mendocino coast is from a vacation resort at Little River. Years ago ten schooners were caught in a storm and wrecked offshore. Timber from this area, loaded onto ships by chute from a mill on the bluff, was used to rebuild San Francisco after the 1906 earthquake.

Opposite page: Crystal Crag rises high above Lake George in California's Mammoth Lakes area. The tree is a Jeffrey pine.

Shasta Dam, 602 feet high and two-thirds of a mile long, utilizes the power of the Sacramento, Pit, and McCloud rivers to produce electricity and to supply water for Central Valley reclamation projects. Shasta reservoir and its 365 miles of shoreline have been incorporated into the Whiskeytown-Shasta-Trinity National Recreation Area. The 14,162-foot dome of Mt. Shasta still wears winter's snow, despite the springtime evidence of flowering redbud.

Upper right: Fishing boats enter Noyo harbor beneath the highway bridge. Noyo is one of the busiest fishing ports on the Pacific Coast.

Reflected in Manzanita Lake is the cone of Lassen Peak. More than 106,000 acres of evergreen forests, about 50 wilderness lakes, 150 miles of trails, and many campgrounds are in Lassen Volcanic National Park. Lassen erupted violently and frequently between 1914 and 1921. It is the southernmost high volcanic peak (elevation 10,457 feet) in the Cascade Range.

Valentine Cave is typical of more than 200 lava caves, or tubes, in Lava Beds National Monument, which was the site of the Modoc Indian War. The cave is 1,500 feet long and was formed when the surface of a lava flow cooled and crusted while the molten interior continued its motion under the crust.

Below: Steam vents, hot springs, mud volcanos, and other thermal activity characterize Bumpass Hell, a spectacular area in Lassen Volcanic National Park. Its elevation is about 8,000 feet, and it is reached by a three-mile round-trip trail hike from Lake Helen on the cross-park highway.

A cloud cap—typical of such high peaks—hovers over the double volcanic cones of Mt. Shasta, described by Joaquin Miller as "lonely as God and white as a winter moon." Shastina, the right-hand cone, is about 12,000 feet high. This view shows the mountain's north side; on the south slopes is a ski area at 8,000 feet elevation.

On preceding page: Shore pines in silhouette—near where the Noyo River flows into the Pacific. California's shoreline Highway 1 bridges the river's mouth.

Opposite page: McArthur-Burney Falls Memorial State Park's 565 acres contain nature trails and picnic sites. Burney Creek drops over a 129-foot lava cliff in a V-shaped twin column of water joined halfway by a curtain of water from hundreds of underground springs. A part of the curtain is shown here.

Under a darkening sky the surf rolls toward the Del Norte coastline. A short distance away, but not shown, are the Jedediah Smith Redwoods.

To separate Oregon and Washington geographically is not easy. They make a fairly neat pair of rectangles that fit together into a larger, fairly neat rectangle divided for the most part by the Columbia River. The greatest natural feature, the topographical event that most determines the character—physically, psychologically, socially, economically, and climatically—of the two states is the Cascade Range. From south to north, it sorts itself out from the jumble of Coast Ranges in northern California and southern Oregon and neatly cuts the Northwest in two (not in half because nearly two-thirds of both states lie to the east of the mountains), depriving the eastern country of the warm Pacific rains, making it semiarid, arid, or even outright desert. The Cascades are themselves cut in two by the legendary "Great River of the West," the relentless Columbia, the only river that, in the millemillenia of geologic time, has managed to wear its way through these mountains and reach the sea.

Flowing from Columbia Lake in the Canadian Rockies, the river makes huge crooked bends through British Columbia and Washington, picking up offerings from many other smaller streams (some of them, like the Yakima, not so small) rimming its own basin. More than 900 miles it flows, almost to Oregon, where it is joined by the prodigious Snake which itself has drained the mountainous landscape for more than 1,000 miles from its beginning in the Grand Tetons of Wyoming. Thus augmented, the Columbia rolls on, separating the states, cleaving the mountains, acquiring still more water from dozens of small streams and from the John Day, the Deschutes, and the Willamette rivers until, 1,232 miles from its commencement, it pours into the Pacific Ocean, having carried a liquid volume many times as great as the Colorado. A great deal, of course, happens to it on the way.

Entering the United States from Canada, the wild river becomes a narrow lake, Franklin D. Roosevelt Lake, 151 miles long. It was created by Grand Coulee Dam, which is in the center of the Coulee Dam National Recreation Area and is the largest concrete structure on earth.

Statistics afford a poor picture, but I will say that the dam is 4,173 feet long, is 550 feet high, and contains 10,585,000 cubic yards of concrete. If it could be weighed, it would tip the scales at 21,600,000 tons. After nine years of work, it was finally finished in 1942, just in time to produce electric power for West Coast defense industries at the beginning of the Second World War. The dam also created Banks Lake, a 25-mile-long body of irrigation and recreation water, occupying the upper part of Grand Coulee itself. A coulee, incidently, means, in western parlance, a canyon or gulch, dry most of the time, created by rainstorms or running water. It also means a flow of lava. Grand Coulee exemplifies both definitions, being the prehistoric course that the Columbia cut through layers and layers of ancient lava. The Columbia passes through ten more dams before it reaches the sea, all of which, downriver from Chief Joseph Dam, have built-in fish ladders or elevators that allow the salmon to leap, swim, or be lifted upstream to spawn.

After The Dalles Dam the river enters the famous gorge it has slowly and inexorably cut, and is still cutting, through the mountain range. Grand and magnificent, the walls of the gorge rise in sheer palisades, and waterfalls plunge over the precipices. There's a booming heroic Wagnerian quality to it all. In fact, it must have reminded some earlier settlers of the Rhine, because on the Washington side they built a little town and called it Bingen after the city in Rhineland-Palatinate (Rheinland-Pfalz).

Emerging from its canyon, the river, studded with islands, spreads out, flows past the environs of the city of Portland, and at Vancouver makes an abrupt curve to the north, then again curves sharply to the west at Longview. In spite of all the dams built upriver to control it, the Columbia still floods in these lower reaches. It is not uncommon, while cruising the river in winter or spring to see whole farms in the low, flat countryside standing knee-deep in water.

The river's mouth is nearly five miles wide, and across it stretches the terrible bar of silt and sand that for years was, and still is, the bane of mariners. Captain Robert Gray, however, in May of 1792 bravely essayed this river mouth in his brig, *Columbia,* naming the river

forthwith. Near the mouth, but tucked back away from the Pacific winds, stands a replica of Fort Clatsop, a national memorial since 1958. There Meriwether Lewis and William Clark spent the winter of 1805-06 after making their historic overland journey from the Mississippi.

Eastern Oregon and Washington, a vast moonscape of high plateaus, mountain ranges, canyons, alkaline lakes, pine forests, and coulees, was once, before irrigation, all dry juniper and sagebrush. Much of it still is. Southeast Oregon remains high desert suitable for cattle and wildlife. South of the isolated town of Burns, at the Malheur National Wildlife Refuge and the Hart Mountain National Antelope Refuge, exotic species of birds and animals may be observed, such as the rare trumpeter swan, the ibis, and of course, antelope. Harney and Malheur lakes, one salt and one fresh, change size considerably with the season, but they provide nesting grounds for birds traveling the Pacific Flyway. The rest of the dry desert country is used for ranching and some lumbering. The people of the High Country tend to be oriented more toward Idaho, since Nampa and Boise are closer than the cities over the mountains. Many people on the coast, Portlanders and Salemites, in spite of the traveling tradition of the West, often dismiss the High Country with a casual remark: "Of course, I've never been in eastern Oregon."

Each September a native phenomenon takes place in eastern Oregon at the town of Pendleton: the Roundup. It is really a get-together, fair, and rodeo after the cattle have been brought down from the High Country for the winter. People come from all over the United States, particularly from Washington, Idaho, and Montana, to drink and play and raise Cain. It's four days of Cadillacs, dirty station wagons, half-ton pickups, pearl-buttoned shirts and Levi's and tooled boots, horses, banners, gonfalons, and Indians. Lots of money changes hands, and a good time is had by all.

North of Pendleton, near Walla Walla, Washington, is the Whitman Mission National Historical Site, the Waiilatpu mission founded by Marcus and Narcissa Whitman in 1836 for the

Oregon / Washington

purpose of educating and Christianizing the Cayuse Indians, who couldn't have been less interested. Eventually the mission became an important and cherished way station on the Oregon Trail. Many a sick and weary emigrant found comfort and rest at the hands of the Whitmans, who were, in the end, killed by the Indians.

The Wallowa Lake area of the Wallowa River valley is the home country of the great Indian chief Joseph of the Nez Percé, who led his people in their last valiant tragic battle against the white man. The valley is in the heart of the Blue and Wallowa mountains, where herds of elk roam today. These mountains occupy the northeast corner of Oregon, and the Blue extend into southeast Washington. They make up a lush and beautiful wilderness full of fish and game and clear streams. Anyone who has experienced the Wallowa country easily understands why the Indians fought so desperately to keep it.

It is here too, that the Snake River cuts its prodigious gorge called Hells Canyon. It's the deepest canyon on the continent (7,900 feet) and is in the process of being dammed. (Although the Snake River project has been roundly "damned" by conservationists, construction proceeds.) The Snake River was not named for its crookedness, but for the name the fur traders gave to the Indians, who, the trappers found, were extremely adept at concealing themselves. In *Fur Hunters of the Far West,* Alexander Ross comments that "They [the Indians] are very appropriately named Snakes."

With the advent of irrigation eastern Washington changed from a desert to a garden. The Yakima and Wenatchee valleys produce millions of dollars' worth of apples, hops, potatoes, and other fruits and vegetables every year. The Columbia Basin is a vast wheat field whose yield is the fifth largest in the country. The center of all this fertility, and the wealth it engenders, is Spokane, Washington's second largest city and capital of what is called The Inland Empire, a wheat, cattle, lumber, and ore-producing region of Washington, Oregon, Idaho, Montana, and Canada. Spokane's not much to look at; it's a banking, commodity, and light-manufacturing town, but it has some pleasant, cool parks that relieve the heat of summer, and the falls of the Spokane River are quite spectacular in the spring, if you can somehow manage to see them. They're right in the middle of town, with buildings on both sides. There are, at the 1970 counting, 170,516 people in Spokane, who, of course, use electricity put out by Coulee Dam. They also utilize—for boating, fishing, hunting, skiing, and hiking—the many fine recreation areas of the Okanogan Highlands and the lovely lake district of Idaho. Spokane is the gateway to both.

The tremendous range of rugged, volcanic mountains that so dramatically divides the climate of the two states took its name from the short, narrow stretch in the Columbia River where the water leaped and rolled over rocks, making navigation of any kind impossible. Lewis and Clark referred to the rough water as cascades, and other travelers called them rapids. They were a major stumbling block on the Oregon Trail and remained so until a road bypassed them, and finally, in 1937, the Bonneville Dam drowned them, making navigation smooth and practicable, as can be seen by the numerous wheat and oil barges that daily ply the river from the interior to the coast. In spite of efforts, mostly by Easterners, to name the mountains the "Presidents' Range," titling individual peaks for ex-presidents—Washington, Adams, Jefferson, and so forth—the trauma of those treacherous river rapids to the spirits of settlers who, after months of heartbreak and travail, found themselves so close to the Promised Land, caused the common name "Cascades" to stick to the whole frustrating range. Though only the Klamath Indians of southern Oregon had a name for the range as a whole— they called them the "mountains of the northern people"—the other native people of the region gave names to the individual peaks, considering them to be gods, and, viewing these mountains even today, it's easy to see why.

Completely different from the Sierras, to which they have no geological relation, the great peaks of the Cascades rise, one by one, lordly and alone, capped with snow—old fire

mountains, cold deities, in a chain from California to Canada, part of the "Circle of Fire" that rings the Pacific Ocean. One of the largest of these peaks, Mt. Mazama, no longer exists as such. The mountaintop, undermined by its own volcanic activity, fell in on itself sometime in the not too distant past, perhaps no more than 7,000 years ago. The huge caldera, or crater, thus formed subsequently filled with water from rain and snow, creating what is now Crater Lake, the deepest lake (1,932 feet) in America.

The Indians of the region must have witnessed the collapse of fiery Mt. Mazama, for their legends, which stand up well with geological explanation, tell of "the Chief of the Below World [who] was driven into his home, and the top of the mountain fell upon him. When the morning sun rose, the high mountain was gone . . . . The rain fell. For many years, the rain fell in torrents and filled the great hole. . . . The Curse of Fire was lifted. Peace and quiet covered the earth."

In 1902 Theodore Roosevelt, an outdoorsman, made Crater Lake a national park. It hasn't been the most frequented of western parks. In 1968 well over twice as many people visited Mt. Rainier, and four times as many stopped by Yosemite. The park's location is awkward for a quick visit, and the country around the lake is not the most beautiful of the Cascades. Some places are barren, forbidding volcanic remains, and other places are unremarkable foothills covered with trees. But the lake! Everyone says the same thing because there's nothing else to say: "You have to see it to believe it." No words, no photograph can re-create what the Indian legend calls simply "peace and quiet," the transcendental tranquility that prevails. And the blue of the water: it has often been explained but never described. Everyone is perfectly right, it has to be seen to be believed.

None of the peaks in the Oregon Cascades are tremendously high, however impressive they may be. The highest in the central range is Mt. Jefferson, less than 11,000 feet. The tallest in the state (11,245 feet) is Mt. Hood. It rises on the south shore of the Columbia, towering sharp and white over the blooming apple, cherry, and pear orchards of the Hood River valley, over the wheat fields of the Wasco country, and over the city of Portland, 45 miles away. Like other glaciated Cascade peaks—McLoughlin, Diamond, The Three Sisters, Washington, Jefferson (some of the presidential names remain)—Mt. Hood takes a heavy load of snow in winter and keeps much of it through the year, making it one of the oldest, busiest, and most popular skiing, climbing, and camping areas in the Northwest. Winter sports also preside across the river at Mt. St. Helens, which rises in an almost perfect snowy cone matching Mt. Hood.

But the biggest mountain of all the Cascades, and the one that so dominates the landscape that it is called by residents of the region simply "The Mountain," is Mt. Rainier, 14,410 feet high. "It is superb in its boldness," says a National Park Service brochure, "rising 11,000 feet in seven miles; one of the world's grand mountains—an arctic island in a temperate zone." The national park that includes the mountain and surrounding ridges and forests was set aside in 1899. Before that, every traveler who saw it was impressed enough to want to name it. The Indians called it Tahoma; Capt. George Vancouver called it Rainier (for his friend and fellow officer in the British navy) when he explored Puget Sound in 1792; and Hall Kelley, the "Boston Schoolmaster," advocating the Presidents' Range idea, wanted to call it Mt. Harrison. Though not erupting, the mountain was active as late as the early 1900s and still emits steam and gases. Once upon a time it was a good 16,000 feet high, but a prehistoric explosion blew the top off, giving it the flattened profile we now see, particularly from the west. The mountain's living glacial system is more extensive and elaborate than any other mountain outside of Alaska, providing perpetually flowing creeks and rivers that pour down the mountainside, cut canyons, make falls, and end up in the Columbia River or Puget Sound.

The mountain also, to employ the favored pun of the locals, is *rainier* than any other place in the Cascades. I have already mentioned the extravagant snowfall the mountain receives; I can add that I have driven from Longmire to

Paradise to Stevens Canyon to White River, back and forth, halfway around the mountain, trying for a week to get a glimpse of its majestic summit through the heavy wads of cloudy rain. Many vacationers on a tour of the West have been disappointed, having failed to find the mountain altogether, just as, often on the same journey, they fail to get a look at the Golden Gate Bridge, hidden in San Francisco's summer fog. When the clouds disperse and the sun comes out, of course, the scene is unsurpassed. At the timberline lie the green, alpine meadows studded with lakes and filled with blue lupine, Indian paintbrush, bear grass, buttercups, and avalanche lilies.

In these high elevations, during July and August after the snow has receded, these flowering meadows most resemble the mythical fields of Elysium. Hiking is a favorite exercise in the park, as are camping and climbing and exploring the ice caves. These days, with climbing schools at the mountain centers demonstrating snow-climbing and ice-climbing techniques, with guided parties and readily rentable climbing equipment, more than 2,000 people, during each four-month climbing season, attain the summit of the mountain; but it's no snap, certainly not as easy as Mt. Whitney, and every now and then somebody is lost in a sudden storm or disappears into a crevasse. The forest streams of the lower elevations provide trout fishing near the campgrounds, some of which are kept open all year. In winter too the road from the park headquarters at Longmire to Paradise Inn at the timberline is kept open whenever possible, and ski tows at Paradise operate on weekends and holidays throughout the season.

In 1968, after 30 years of off-and-on consideration, Congress finally authorized over 1,000 square miles of the wild, northern Cascades as a national park. Divided into four parts, the preserve includes the Ross Lake National Recreation Area, a north and a south wilderness unit, and the Lake Chelan National Recreation Area. The Ross area follows the gorge of the Skagit River, which, with dams and resultant lakes, can be used for boating and fishing. The area is accessible from the west by paved road. (An extension of this road

to the other side of the mountains over Rainy Pass is under construction.) The north unit is without roads, and the south unit has only a few miles of them. There are no accommodations, no swimming (the water's too cold), and no skiing, but there are all those square miles of unspoiled, uncrowded mountains for those who like to backpack, hike, climb, and explore wilderness trails that others seldom pursue.

Unlike the rest of the Cascade Range, the northern mountains are not volcanic in origin, except for scattered peaks. Their present rugged, jagged shapes were formed by glacial action. Lake Chelan, the headwater of which extends into the national recreation area in the south of the new park, is a long narrow glacial trough, presenting the closest approximation of a fjord in the Pacific states. Boats regularly serve the lake from Chelan (near the Columbia River) to Stehekin at the other end. It's a beautiful trip and presently is the only access to the park from the east. On that side of the mountain axis the weather is warm and dry, and the country is correspondingly less interesting. On the western side, however, the wet side, be prepared for lots of rain, lots of fog, many storms, and lots of general miserable overcast any time of the year. Of course, when the weather clears, it's gorgeous.

From south to north, the Coast Range from the California border narrows considerably along the western edge of Oregon and Washington. The mountains are low, seldom more than 5,000 feet high, but in typical Coast Range fashion, they are very rough, at least as far as southwest Washington, where they spread out and level off before rising again to form the picturesque welter of miniature Himalayas, the Olympic Mountains.

At their southern limits in Oregon, in the Siskiyous, or I should say, *under* the Siskiyous, is the Oregon Cave, the "Marble Halls of Oregon," as Joaquin Miller called it. Officially it's called the Oregon Caves National Monument, even though it consists of but a single cave of several chambers and passages of marbleized limestone, damp and baroque, with dripping calciferous stone shapes remindful of the architectural extravagances of Gaudí.

From the Siskiyous the Coast Range edges

the shoreline northward, producing dozens of streams and short rivers. The longest of these is probably the Umpqua, which rises near Crater Lake and joins the sea at Reedsport. (For anyone quiet enough within himself, who appreciates fresh water, a moving stream, a moderate climate, and a tranquil pastoral existence, and who doesn't mind the rain, the valley of the lower Umpqua would be his heart's desire.)

Other rivers—the Rogue (beloved for its white water by rubber-boat and kayak enthusiasts), the Coquille, the Smith, the Siuslaw, the Alsea, the Yaquina, the Nestucca, the Nehalem—are all logging rivers. With the forests of the Blue Mountains, the stands of pine, the seemingly endless and unbroken woods of the Cascade and Coast ranges, Oregon possesses the largest supply of sawtimber in the nation. Lumbering, with all its attendant industries, remains the state's biggest business.

On the coast, the Coos Bay and North Bend area is the center of the trade, while over the mountains, Roseburg, Eugene, Salem and—well, hardly a town, city, or village exists that doesn't have a mill. The lower Willamette and both sides of the lower Columbia are lined with them. Pulp plants, plywood factories, and pressed board, hardboard, cardboard, wood, and wood-product manufacturing of all kinds extend right on across the river and up to Puget Sound, in fact, to Canada. It's a colorful industry—lumberjacks and big saws, tugboats guiding huge log booms down the mountain rivers—but it's also a destructive one. Though many of the really big lumber companies now grow trees as a crop, selectively cutting and scientifically "farming" their vast holdings, many others do not, so that much of the timber being cut will never be replaced, and the slopes, thus denuded, immediately compound the horrendous ecological and economic hazards of fire, erosion, and flood. At the same time, the factories and mills, virtually uncontrolled, pollute the air with chemicals and noxious smells.

United States Highway 101 is a dark, sinuous ribbon that strings together the gigantic rocks and headlands, the sand dunes (a movement is under way to make the Oregon Dunes between Coos Bay and Florence a national seashore) and driftwood beaches, the lighthouse points, the green bridges and blue bays, the sea-cut caves and arches, and all the little fishing ports of the Oregon coast. Fishing and fish canning are still important industries in Oregon and Washington, in spite of a general decline. The Russians and the Japanese, who are wholesale ocean predators, fish with scientific efficiency off the Northwest Coast and seasonally deplete the domestic supply, while man's irresistible encroachments upon the wild country—the building of dams, the taming, commercialization, and clogging of streams with agricultural and industrial waste—have alarmingly reduced the population of salmon, the king fish of the Northwest.

Astoria, at the head of the Coast Range where the Columbia cuts through, once John Jacob Astor's fur-trading post, is the main port for the fish-canning industry. Crabs, oysters, other shellfish, tuna, are taken on these shores, oysters especially in Washington's Willapa and Grays bays and in Puget Sound, but there again, the oysters are disappearing. But, to add a cheerful note, the Dungeness crab, the big, fine, fat crab that everybody loves to eat with drawn butter or served up cold with sharp mayonnaise, seems to be doing well.

The valley of the Willamette River and the low country north of the Columbia to Olympia, Washington's capital at the head of Puget Sound, between the Coast Range and the Cascades, bring to mind another valley between mountains: the Central Valley of California. But what a difference! It's not just their sizes (the Northwest valleys are not nearly as big as the Central Valley which, as I have said, is a great big, monotonous, crop machine filled with nondescript towns); it's the countryside itself. To be sure, the Willamette Valley grows crops, many crops—prunes, berries, grass seed, hops, walnuts, filberts, holly, daffodils—in very rich soil, but there is no monotony, and the towns present their own singular images. Past them, the Willamette River, carrying logging and towboat traffic, wanders and curves placidly through the low undulant hills and flatlands, joined frequently by smaller streams that flow from the forested mountains on either side. There are still some ferries and covered

bridges on some of those streams, and some swimming holes, and tall shade trees around white frame farmhouses with strong, red barns. August comes on hot and exudes the dry, languid smell of deep summer. And the cottonwoods turn yellow in the fall. The white settlers of the valley were Easterners, New Englanders, many of them—it was Eugene F. Skinner of Essex County, New York, who laid out Eugene; and Albany, Salem, and Portland are not Indian names—and they used the valley well and thriftily, as do the inhabitants today.

In the intermontane corridor from Medford and Ashland in the south to Portland in the north, live three-quarters of Oregon's people. Except for Eastern Oregon College at La Grande, all the state's major institutions of higher learning are located there, including the

University of Oregon at Eugene, Oregon State University at Corvallis, Portland State University, Willamette University in Salem, which is, of course, the state capital. Salem has grown considerably in the last ten years; new highways have been built, and new bridges completed across the Willamette; but in spite of such physical growth the town has stayed much the same. It's still an agricultural hub (fruit and berries); some of the old elaborate Victorian houses remain; the state penitentiary is still there; the state capitol grounds contiguous with the grassy campus of Willamette University, with its old brick buildings, ivy-covered halls, and shade trees, still make a pleasant and sheltered oasis in the middle of downtown; and the university students still fidget restlessly on their off-hours. There's not too much to do in Salem. Of course, you can always go to Portland, but then, there's not too much to do there either, not if you're that young.

Portland has grown comparatively little in population (10,000 in ten years), but it's by far the largest and most important urban center in the state and one of the two major cities and seaports in the northwestern United States (Seattle, of course, is the other). The city grew from a clearing on the west side of the Willamette, where, in 1845, Amos Lovejoy, from Massachusetts, and Francis Pettygrove, from Maine, having staked out some acres on the banks of the river, tossed a coin to see what they would call it. One wanted Boston, the other Portland. Pettygrove won. In 1970 the population was 382,619, but as some contented residents say, it retains much of the charm and ambience of a small town. Others find it all too citified. They regret the freeways which first took the fine old western-style buildings along the waterfront and then, just recently, cut through the heart of the city, taking still more venerable residences and churches. "Those of us who protested the freeway," says Stewart Holbrook, "were drowned out by the clamor of businessmen shouting that we were impeding progress." The old west side of Portland possesses most of the city's amenities, such as the few fine seafood restaurants, the theaters and hotels, the excellent public library and art museum, and the superb views of the valleys of the rivers and Cascades (from Council Crest on a clear day you can see five of the great snowcapped peaks of the range—Hood, Adams, St. Helens, Jefferson, and Rainier). The west side also has most of the city parkland and the choice residential districts.

Portland is called the "City of Roses," and roses and other flowers do grow beautifully in the moderate climate. Every June the city holds a Rose Festival which draws many tourists and makes the cash registers ring downtown. There's a parade with a "rose queen" and baton twirlers, Legion band, and cowboys on horseback—all the usual things, including an honored "celebrity." It's a businessmen's affair, and many of the older residents, even those who grow roses, turn up their noses at some of the goings-on. Portland is also the center of a large shipping and manufacturing region which includes the pulp and paper mills of Oregon City; the river trade in grain and produce from the Columbia Basin and the Willamette Valley; and the aluminum plant, textile mills, and shipyards of Vancouver across the Columbia in Washington. The interstate bridges of the Pacific Highway (Interstate 5) closely link Portland and Vancouver, which is the site of old Fort Vancouver, now a national historic site and once headquarters of the Hudson's Bay Company, the fur capital, social capital, cultural capital, agricultural capital of the Northwest. The fort, partially restored at present, was presided over for many years by John McLoughlin ("White Eagle" to the Indians, "Father of Oregon" to later historians), whose name, along with that of Captain Vancouver himself, pervaded and still pervades the territory.

Though the residents of Washington are spread throughout the state more generally than are Oregon's, by far the greatest numbers are concentrated in the valleys north from Vancouver to Longview to Olympia then along the east shore of Puget Sound to Tacoma, Seattle, Everett, and Bellingham.

The world of the Sound is a world of water. Seattle is surrounded by it and drenched with it much of the year. During the summer months, especially during July, the city usually dries off, and the sun gets hot. Then the damp in-

habitants rush to the lakeshore or take to their boats, or head for the hills which, like the sparkling northern blue waters of the Sound, are practically next door. Few of the world's cities (one of the few would be Oslo, which resembles Seattle in many ways) can provide so many adjacent escapes to the great outdoors.

In recent years the city has also been paying more attention to amenities within its own limits. After the World's Fair of 1962, a permanent Seattle Center was established, which is connected by monorail to the downtown. Besides the inescapable Space Needle, with its full-circle view of everything, including Mt. Rainier, when the skies are clear, the Seattle Center offers an amusement park, a sports center, a science center, recreation centers for young and old (none for the man in the middle, who, presumably, is too busy to play), an opera house, an art museum, and a theater. To my mind, the most pleasurable diversion within the city is still the old Pike Place Market, the last indigenous open market on the Coast and maybe, even, in the country (fancied-up places such as the Farmers Market in Los Angeles don't qualify). The agglomeration of races and foods and merchandise, the colors and smells, and the clamor of many tongues—all those things we have come to associate with markets of the old style, where the fruits and vegetables came in last night and the fish swam this morning—are all there for as long as it lasts.

In the somewhat academic rivalry between Portland and Seattle, Portland claims age, and Seattle pulls rank. After all, Portland was a well-established social and cultural community when Seattle was a muddy logging camp, but Seattle has grown to be the biggest (well over half a million people in 1970), and it handles a larger share of ocean commerce, especially to Alaska and to Japan and the rest of the Far East. But Portland's economy is more stable, and the satisfied mood of the city reflects it. Seattle's biggest industry over all is Boeing, the gargantuan aerospace complex of research and development. When Boeing is fat and prosperous and flying high, so is Seattle, but when Boeing is grounded, the whole city is down. At this writing, the skies are clouded, the outlook damp and gloomy, but as with the weather,

the rain may pass, the clouds may part, and the great hoary god Rainier may rise up to the very sun. It's a happy time in Seattle when one man can say to another on the street, "Look, you can see the Mountain today."

West of Seattle, beyond the green labyrinth of wooded islands in the Sound, stands an unlikely, undomesticated, unique range of little mountains—as I said before, a miniature Himalaya—the Olympics. As the final extrusion of the Coast Range in this country, they form much of Olympic National Park. Though none of the peaks reach 8,000 feet, they rise directly from sea level to a stormy crest of heaving glaciers, often obscured by vapors. I remember, however, one winter midnight while standing lookout on the bow of a freighter entering the Strait of Juan de Fuca when there were no clouds, when the mountains, like the mountains East of the Sun and West of the Moon, cold, white, implacable in the icy moonlight, watched us pass by. Even on sunny days they seem exotic, foreign, like the mountains of another country far away.

There's more to the park than mountains: there is a stretch of seashore that is probably the only remaining primitive shoreline on the Pacific, there are quiet lakes, and there are the rain forests. Fed perpetually—by the rain in winter, the melting glaciers and snow in summer—the rivers (the Quinault, the Queets, the Hoh) pour off the western Olympic slopes into low, fecund valleys, where the forest community is so thick and crowded that life must grow upon life. Here the Douglas fir, the treasure tree of the Northwest, and the hemlock and the red cedar reach their ultimate dimensions, their trunks covered and their branches dripping with half a dozen kinds of moss. Moss grows upon moss; vine entendrils vine. A fallen Sitka spruce disappears in a swamp of deer fern, sword fern, licorice fern. Vine maple fills the spaces between the trunks of the mammoth trees and filters whatever sunlight makes its way through the jungle above. Though Mt. Waialeale in the state of Hawaii is the wettest place (almost 40 *feet* of rain a year) in the United States, this Olympic forest is the wettest place on the Pacific Coast, a long, long way from Bagdad in the desert of California.

The lava pinnacles of Haystack Rock and the Needles, viewed during a lull in a winter storm, are most familiar of the thousands of "stacks" along the coast. Cannon Beach's Haystack Rock is more than 250 feet high. An old cannon washed ashore from a wrecked ship gave the beach its name. It is about 85 miles from Portland.

Joaquin Miller Chapel contains stalactites and pillars and canopies of limestone beneath a domed ceiling in Oregon Caves National Monument adjacent to Siskiyou National Forest. Miller called the caves the "Marble Halls of Oregon."

Wizard Island rises nearly 700 feet above the surface of Crater Lake, a lake so beautiful, states author Kentfield, "You must see it to believe it." Some idea of its size can be gained by noting the wake left by a 60-foot passenger boat just beyond the island.

Below: The time, early morning in autumn. Place, along the Siuslaw River near the Oregon coast.

Upper left: The Willamette River flows 200 miles through a valley that is the largest concentrated natural agricultural area in the Northwest. It also has an annual salmon run. *Upper middle:* The Siuslaw River is in a small Coast Range valley of farms and sawmills, and tides from the Pacific affect its flow for miles. *Upper right:* Remote Three Sisters Wilderness in the Cascades had several periods of volcanism. LeConte Crater and Wickiup Plains are in the foreground. The lava flow at South Sister's base is called Rock Mesa. The Sisters, all over 10,000 feet high, are also of another volcanic period. *Below:* A mile of sand dunes extends from the sea to freshwater Cleawox Lake in Honeyman State Park, named for Jessie M. Honeyman. She helped beautify Oregon's highways and roadsides. Oregon leads in state park development.

Upper right: The jagged volcanic spires of Smith Rocks rise above Crooked River. From this point, 1,000 feet above Smith Rock State Park, which has 605 acres of cliffs and river canyon, can be seen all of the Cascade Range's high peaks in Oregon and even some in Washington. Snowcaps visible are Bachelor Butte, Broken Top, and the Three Sisters. Irrigated farms surround Smith Rocks.

Lower right: A spiral drive goes to the 5,010-foot summit crater of Lava Butte in central Oregon. Nearby is Lava River Caves State Park. This volcanic region, resembling the moon's surface, has been used by space personnel for study and practice.

Left: Steep headlands and cliffs and crescent beaches are typical of north central Oregon's coast. This primitive area, near a village called Roads End, is reached by hiking or at times by boat. US 101 is a few miles inland.

On preceding page left: Mt. Jefferson Wilderness Area, dominated by the mountain, is reached only by trail. So is the lake, unnamed, on the crest of the Cascade Range. It is one of a cluster of lava and tree-fringed lakes called Papoose Lakes. They are in the western edge of the Warm Springs Indian Reservation, which adjoins the Mt. Jefferson Wilderness Area.

On preceding page right: The Crooked River, from its headwaters in the Ochoco Mountains, mostly flows through a deep lava-walled canyon. This peninsula of sandstone cliffs and pinnacles is Smith Rocks; its state park is not shown.

Above: Small (13 acres) Painted Hills State Park is one of several parks in the foothills of the Ochoco Mountains. This part of central Oregon, nine miles northwest of Mitchell, is rangeland, and cattle graze at will over the eroded Painted Hills.

Upper right: Early morning ground fog occurs frequently during autumn. The picture was taken from Cape Foulweather, at Otter Crest State Wayside Park, which is between Newport and Oceanlake on US 101.

Blue flag, or wild iris

Bear grass

Wallflower

In Silver Falls State Park more than a dozen waterfalls of from 15 feet to almost 200 feet in height are reached by trails lined with moss-covered maple trees. Here the trail passes directly behind the water of Lower South Falls.

Thunderheads build high above the dome of South Sister peak, which looms over Sparks Lake in the forested central Cascades.

On preceding page: Chanticleer Point, from where the picture was taken, is about 800 feet above the Columbia River. Crown Point Vista House is in the middle distance. Highways and railroads follow the water-level route on both sides of the river.

Left: Overlooking the Columbia River and right next to the Columbia River Highway is Multnomah Falls, whose plunge is 620 feet from Larch Mountain in the Cascades.

Right: In this view from the crest of Cape Kiwanda can be seen (center left) Nestucca Bay and the mouth of the Nestucca River. During the summer, sportsmen and commercial fishermen launch their boats from the beach in the foreground to catch salmon offshore.

Portland has an enviable location in the valley near the Willamette River's confluence with the Columbia. Its residents living on the range of west hills in the city can view five snowcapped mountains in clear weather. Mt. Hood, under the full moon, is 40 miles away.

The rich farmland of the valley of the Tualatin River, which is a relative of the much larger Willamette River, is slowly being taken over by suburban developments from Portland. To the left is Mt. Rainier, more than 100 miles distant; Mt. St. Helens is the symmetrical volcanic cone; and Mt. Adams is at the extreme right—all are in Washington.

Salmon River is a short but vigorous river with waterfalls and white water rapids that race down the foothills of the Cascade Range near Mt. Hood. The picture was taken outside Mt. Hood National Forest from US 26. The trees are native big-leaf maples.

Left: Wahkeena Falls is 30 miles east of Portland on old Columbia River Highway. It is in Mt. Hood National Forest and almost a mile from Multnomah Falls.

The rhythm of the surf is hypnotic; the beauty of a wholly natural scene, such as at Cape Kiwanda, becomes powerful—together they generate an experience that is personally revelatory. "Fortunately for us," says Ray Atkeson, "and especially for future generations, more people—including highway engineers—are becoming actively involved with the ecology and the preservation of the 'good earth.' "

The volcanic cone of Mt. Adams, in Washington, as seen from the crest of Oregon's Larch Mountain. In the foreground are fireweed blossoms.

Upper: The Wallowa Mountains in northeastern Oregon rise abruptly from Enterprise (3,757 feet) to the Eagle Cap Wilderness. The Snake River separates the Wallowas from the Seven Devils Range in Idaho. Cattle and hay, with some timber harvesting, are the area's main products. Lakes and peaks in the wilderness have elevations of from 8,000 to 10,000 feet.

Below: The Punch Bowl on Eagle Creek in the Cascades lies in a very wild area. A trail, 2½ miles from Columbia River Highway, parallels the stream's entire length. A state salmon hatchery is at the creek's confluence with the Columbia, near Bonneville Dam.

Opposite page: Munson Falls is 319 feet high and located in the Coast Range foothills, one mile east of US 101 near the city of Tillamook.

Sunlight, filtered by autumn clouds, touches the grass-covered rocks and · the water of the lower Umpqua River in western Oregon's Coast Range.

Oneonta Gorge apparently was created when a stream followed a fracture in the volcanic crust of the Cascade mountain that rises above the Columbia River. The gorge is several hundred feet deep, and sunlight reaches into its depths for less than an hour each day.

Mt. Hood, whose 11,245 feet makes it the highest peak in Oregon, is seen from a timber area northwest of the mountain in the McGee Creek watershed. Vine maple, in autumn colors, contrasts with the second-growth forest of evergreen trees.

Wheat is one of Oregon's principal food crops. Wasco County, where this picture was taken, is one of five counties that have nearly a million acres of wheatland. Probably half of this acreage is planted in wheat each year, and in the next year lies fallow (note the fields at right) or is used for rotating crops. Most of the state's wheat is ''soft wheat,'' much of which is exported.

Cape Disappointment is at the mouth of the Columbia River, where countless ships
have come to grief on spits of sand that jut into the sea. However, the hazard has been
lessened recently by construction of rock jetties north and south of the river's mouth.
The picture was taken from 1,666-acre Fort Canby State Park in Washington.

Above: Glenwood Valley is a farming and ranching area near Mt. Adams. Although
the elevation is comparatively low on the eastern slopes of the Cascades, deep snow
covers the valley for long periods during winter.

Some of the largest bulb fields in America are in southwestern Washington; others
are in the Puyallup Valley and the Skagit Valley in the Puget Sound region.
These daffodils are blooming near Woodland.

Mt. St. Helens, with a cloud capping its 9,677-foot peak, and Spirit Lake at its base form one of the world's most beautiful mountain settings. Several youth camps and public campgrounds are located along the lake's 12-mile timbered shoreline.

The timberline trees are veiled by clouds. This alpine meadow
filled with wild flowers at Cloudy Pass is in the center
of Glacier Peak Wilderness Area and is reached only by trail.

The Red Delicious is the most abundant variety of apple grown in irrigated Yakima Valley, which together with distant Wenatchee Valley claims to be the apple capital of the world.

Right: Mt. Adams, 12,307 feet in elevation, is the second highest—next to Mt. Rainier—mountain in the Northwest. It is in Gifford Pinchot National Forest and is viewed here from the shore of Takhlakh Lake.

Far right: In the more than 80,000 acres of Goat Rocks Wilderness, many small streams, of which this one is typical, start from springs or melting snowfields and gain size and dash when joined by others from alpine meadows and forests. The wilderness is in the Cascade Range.

Below: Klickitat Valley lies between the Columbia Hills outlining these poplar trees and Horse Heaven Hills. Although this farming valley which surrounds the town of Goldendale is less than 2,000 feet higher than the Columbia River, deep snows often accumulate and farmers and ranchers here, as in other communities in eastern Washington, prefer to work their spreads from homes in a nearby town.

On preceding page: Shortly after the Columbia River flows through lava-walled Wallula Gap, shown here, it becomes the boundary between Washington and Oregon. McNary Dam slows the river perceptibly. The lava pillars (upper right in picture) are sometimes called The Captains. Sand dunes are created by winds blowing through the gap.

Right: Mt. Rainier, the "Monarch of the Northwest," is 14,410 feet high. Paradise Valley is accessible all year by highway, which is kept open in winter by snowplows.

Upper left: Palouse Falls has formed a canyon of its own making in the great lava flows of eastern Washington. The falls, in a 95-acre park of that name, are nearly 200 feet high. A few miles below the falls the most ancient remains of man on this continent were found in the canyon a few years ago. The archaeological area has since been drowned by the backwater from Lower Monumental Dam on the Snake River, in seeming contradiction to John Donne's claim that "every man is a peece of the Continent."

Lower left: The ice caves in Mt. Rainier's Paradise Glacier, created by the flow of air and water beneath the glacier, undergo continuous change. They are reached by trail: a five-mile round trip and a climb of a few thousand feet from Paradise Valley.

Above: Steptoe Butte is more than 1,000 feet above the surrounding Palouse (rolling hills) grainfields north of Colfax. The butte is a pre-Cambrian peak rising through the Columbia River plateau basalt, a vast lava flow which covered eastern Washington 15 million years ago but which did not inundate peaks (steptoes) that date back 500 million years. The Palouse region is the world's richest wheat-producing land.

Upper left: Now under irrigation in the Columbia Basin Reclamation area are 513,000 acres producing sugar beets, potatoes, corn, and hay. Some lakes have been developed for recreational use, plus reservoirs from which water is sent to such farmland as this hayfield.

Left: This beach near Point Grenville is in the Quinalt Indian Reservation near Highway 109 in the southwestern part of the Olympic Peninsula.

The first Tacoma Narrows Bridge between Tacoma and the Kitsap Peninsula was flapped to destruction in 1940 by a violent windstorm. The present bridge was opened to traffic in 1950 and is 5,450 feet long, its main span 2,800 feet, and is 184 feet above water. Mt. Rainier is in the distance beyond Tacoma.

The beautiful port city of Seattle, on Elliot Bay in Puget Sound, has three lakes within its boundary: Lake Washington, Lake Union, and Green Lake. Greater Seattle includes Tacoma and Everett.

Snoqualmie Falls is 268 feet high and is located on the Snoqualmie River between its pass and Seattle. A public park is at the top of the falls.

Kachess Lake in the background is over ten miles long. Log trucks in the Cascades sometimes make 100-mile hauls to the mills.

Right: Hemlocks line the shore of Picture Lake near the foot of Mt. Shuksan, which is in North Cascades National Park. The foreground area is outside the park.

This scene is near Leavenworth, where the Wenatchee River flows from the Cascade mountains into the Wenatchee Valley.

Above: Remote but popular with mountain climbers, Mt. Eldorado (8,868 feet) is covered with glaciers on all its slopes. Many miles of hiking are needed to reach it. The north, or back, side of Eldorado is much more rugged than this the south side, seen here across a slope of flowering lupine on Sahale Arm in North Cascades National Park.

Upper right: These crests and valleys can be seen from the highway between Port Angeles and Hurricane Ridge in Olympic National Park. The highway climbs from sea level to nearly 6,000 feet in less than 20 miles.

Lower right: Lake Crescent, at the foot of Mt. Storm King, is several miles long. It lies in a mountain-bound pocket of Olympic National Park only a few hundred feet above the level of the nearby Strait of Juan de Fuca.

A series of huge power dams from Bonneville to Grand Coulee utilize the Columbia River;
they've created great lakes which reach from dam to dam. Here, near Northport, just south of the Canadian border,
the Columbia flows free, not yet reaching the upper end of Franklin D. Roosevelt Lake,
which extends downstream 151 miles to Grand Coulee Dam.

Club mosses especially favor native and vine maple trees. The rain forest in Olympic National Park, watered extravagantly by precipitation from the nearby Pacific, includes cedar, alder, hemlock, fir, spruce, and various other trees.

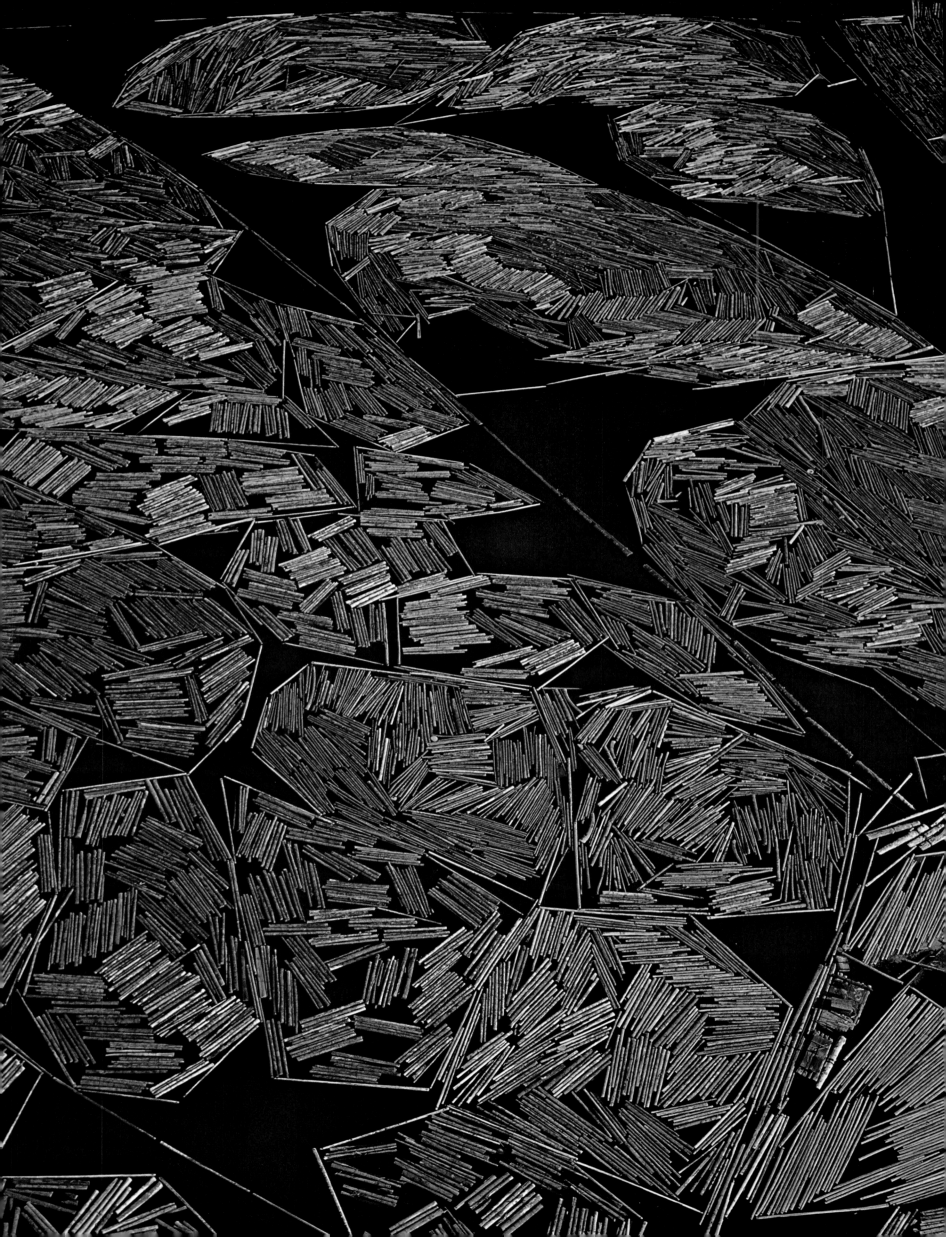

Thousands of logs are held in booms in the harbor of Port Angeles, awaiting the needs of mills that produce lumber, paper, and other wood products. The harbor is unique. A natural peninsula, narrow Ediz Hook, loops out and into the Strait of Juan de Fuca and almost encloses the bay. A large ferryboat carries travelers between Port Angeles and Victoria, British Columbia.

Deception Pass State Park encompasses 1,767 acres on several of the San Juan Islands in Puget Sound. The picture was taken from near the campground on Whidbey Island.

At the timberline on Kulshan Ridge in Mt. Baker National Forest, an early autumn snow has fallen. Winter snows often reach 30 feet in depth and provide exceptional skiing for about nine months of the year. In the distance, clouds roll across valleys and ridges of the Cascade Range.

Right: Up in northern Washington, almost on the Canadian line, is Kulshan Ridge, which offers an unexcelled view of Mt. Baker. Kulshan was the Indian name for Mt. Baker.

Lower right: The overall length of Grand Coulee Dam is four-fifths of a mile, and Franklin D. Roosevelt Lake, created by the dam and now part of Coulee Dam National Recreation Area, has 660 miles of shoreline. In addition to the power that is generated, twelve 65,000-horsepower pumps lift water 280 feet from Roosevelt Lake to Banks Lake, where the water irrigates half a million acres of land in central Washington. Eventually the Columbia Basin Project will double the area under irrigation.

A number of hanging glaciers in the Picket Range feed their melt water into Luna Lake, which is in a glacial moraine. This is a very remote scene. The Pickets, two ranges of serrated and glaciered peaks, are in the heart of North Cascades National Park, which comprises 570,000 acres of the Cascade Range.

Geographically British Columbia and the states of Washington and Oregon are much the same. This Canadian province too is met by the Pacific. It too has wet coastal areas with spectacular mountains, range after range paralleling the sea—the Coast Mountains, with massive Mt. Fairweather (15,300 feet), and Cariboo, Monashee, Selkirk, and Purcell in the Columbia Mountains—following one after another, interspersed with plateaus and valleys and cut by the cold mountain streams in their flow to the sea. Finally, to the east, beyond the mountains which catch the clouds, lies an interior area of dry plains

This is a vast land—larger than California, Washington, and Oregon together—with rugged wilderness, magnificent fjords, and untamed rivers. It has grandeur, and its size gives it a natural immunity to penetration—the wilderness remains alone, for the people cluster mainly in the southwest, along the irrigated river valleys and on scenic, flowered Vancouver Island.

Of the beautiful towns in the huge province, two have through the years achieved considerable eminence—Victoria and Vancouver.

Victoria, the provincial capital of British Columbia, originally (1843) Fort Victoria, was, according to Canadian Coast Guard Captain John T. Walbran writing in 1908, "named by the officers of the Hudson's Bay Company after Her late revered Majesty Queen Victoria, who in 1837 had succeeded to the British Crown; born 24 May 1819, at Kensington Palace, and died 22 January, 1901, at Osborne, Isle of Wight." The city has remained steadfastly British and securely provincial ever since. Though some of the home country nostalgia has worn off (traffic is no longer directed by London-type "bobbies"), afternoon tea is still a flourishing institution (and rightly so, it seems to me, for as Algernon says in *The Importance of Being Earnest,* it's customary for civilized people to take some sustenance at four o'clock). Many a small retirement cottage with a flagpole and a dooryard full of hollyhocks and roses overlooking the sea bears on its picket gate, not *Mon Repos* or *Dunroamin',* but *Trafalgar* or *Suez* or *Calcutta.*

Victoria is a pretty town, a hospitable one, a self-confident one, and though traffic and tourism increase annually, a quiet one. Besides the buildings of the Provincial Parliament, the most interesting and imposing structure in town is the Empress Hotel, smack in the middle of the city. An endlessly rambling late-Victorian structure of lofty ceilings and stained glass, it opens from lobby to lobby to sun rooms to writing rooms to afternoon rooms to orangeries to enclosed gardens to swimming baths to outer gardens to. . . . It's operated by the Canadian Pacific Railway, and a traveler need entertain no thought of putting up at any place other than the Empress.

Another sprawling place, north of Victoria, is the old Butchart mansion, surrounded by an estate planted over the years with increasingly more elaborate gardens. This is a tourist attraction, and you pay to get in, but anyone who delights in flowers or who wonders at the anomaly of such a venture being initiated on the rough wild Northwest frontier will not hesitate to visit it. There are an elegant, formal Italian garden, a Japanese garden, a rock garden, and, of course, a rose garden with thousands of bushes and hundreds of varieties with names like those of race horses—Black Beauty, Scarlet George, Pink Pacer— that rose growers give their thoroughbreds.

Though Victoria, on Vancouver Island, is the capital of British Columbia, Vancouver, on the mainland, is by far the largest city in the province, and it seems to get larger every time you turn around. It had over 410,000 people in 1966, and I wouldn't be surprised if it tops half a million in a few years. Its position in relation to Canada is much the same as that of Vladivostok to the Soviet Union—the only deepwater, year-round, Pacific coast port with rail and road connections to the vast interior of the dominion. No bar or reef obstructs the harbor, Burrard Inlet, which the ubiquitous Captain Vancouver named for Sir Harry Burrard, Bart., Groom of the Bedchamber to George III, Lord of the Admiralty. (Vancouver's generosity toward his buddies in the service was almost flagrant. As stated earlier, he gave the mountain the name of Admiral Rainier, and the Sound he bestowed upon his own second

British Columbia

lieutenant, Peter Puget.) Vancouver described the harbor when he first entered it in June, 1792: "The shores in this situation were formed by steep rocky cliffs that afforded no convenient space for pitching our tent, which compelled us to sleep in the boats. Some of the young gentlemen, however, preferring the stony beach for their couch, without duly considering the high water mark, found themselves incommoded by the flood tide, of which they were not apprized until nearly afloat; and one of them slept so soundly that I believe he might have been conveyed to some distance had he not been awakened by his companions." Today, ships of all nations and sizes pass in and out of Sir Harry's inlet, including the great P. & O. liners from Australasia.

Next to San Francisco, Vancouver is physiographically the most beautiful city on the Pacific Coast. Nearly surrounded by water and backed up immediately by the snowcapped peaks of the Coast Mountains, it should for maximum effect be approached first by sea. That way you pass by the green forests of Stanley Park and pass under the elegant Lions Gate Bridge, that connects the city with its suburbs to the north. It's a short walk from the docks to town, and in spite of the size of the place, most of the services a traveler requires are within a few blocks of each other. In that respect it maintains a British character. As for the rest, it's thoroughly American. A superabundance, almost an embarrassment, of hydroelectric power enables buildings—many new high-rises of which the city is very proud —to be lighted full blast inside and out all night long.

Many of its citizens express apprehension that Vancouver is growing too fast (there has not been such a boom since gold was discovered along the Fraser River, the mouth of which, by the way, forms the southern limits of the city), but there seems to be no slowing it down. Sooner or later it may have to pay the piper; many Edens have been despoiled by energy and blind optimism, to say nothing of greed, but that's a human problem, not a geographical one. Humanistically, Vancouver has moved out of the wilderness. It now sponsors a fine International Arts Festival; and it has built, not quite but almost, overnight one of the most creditable, most amenable, and most contemporaneously beautiful universities in North America. (Compare it, for instance, with the University of California at Irvine, also contrived out of whole cloth but put together in stale Los Angeles-department-store style.)

Beyond Vancouver, the Coast Mountains continue, growing higher, more remote, wilder. The snow falls, the rivers run, the rain pours down the mountainsides. There's plenty of water there, and someday, surely, there will be people.

These grainfields lie in Bulkley River valley near Telkwa, British Columbia.

The Englishman River flows down a series of waterfalls into a deep rockbound
gorge in Englishman River Park. The park is on Vancouver Island.

The crests of glacier-clad Tantalus Range ride above the fog in a deep valley.
The view is from an alpine meadow in Garibaldi Provincial Park.

Upper: The Sunken Garden area of Butchart Gardens is where the first plantings were made many years ago in an abandoned lime quarry. The famous gardens are near Victoria on Vancouver Island.

Left: Long Beach extends into the distance from the forested headland and offshore rocks in new Wickaninnish Beach Park. The park is on the west coast of Vancouver Island.

Upper right: This panorama of Vancouver is seen from the crest of Grouse Mountain, nearly 4,000 feet above the city. An aerial tramway and chair lifts carry passengers directly to the top from North Vancouver.

Above: At nightfall the Parliament building is brightened by thousands of lights. The pleasure boats are anchored in Victoria Harbor.

Left: Flower baskets hanging from lampposts throughout the heart of Victoria are a friendly and distinctive feature of this city. In the background is the Provincial Parliament Building.

Epilogue

In the winter of 1970–71 the heaviest snowfall in nearly 20 years was laid in on the Sierra Nevada. Donner Summit, the notorious pass, was closed. Wind and drifting snow had rendered the most efficient mechanized equipment (snowplows and snow-clearing machines) helpless. The Southern Pacific had managed, momentarily, to clear its tracks; but Interstate 80, the much extolled, all-weather superroad, was closed even to those motorists with chains; and more snow was to come.

Television newsman from Sacramento to snowplow operator surveying his equipment buried in white powder at Donner Pass: "What's the trouble here? In your opinion."

Operator (Incredulously): "Well, it's the snow. We can't git the plow out. We can't git nothin' movin'."

Newsman: "What are you going to do?"

Operator: "I guess we dig 'em out by hand. (Giggles). Hope we don't git no more snow."

Long shot, zoom in. A man and a woman with shovels on the peak of their A-frame digging out their chimney, wind sending snow-spray off the crest of their roof.

Western Oregon and Washington were blasted with winds up to 175 miles an hour. Tillamook and Clatsop counties (coastal counties) were designated disaster areas. Rain was cascading down the mountainsides and rushing through the rivers to the sea. Flooding was imminent. Then, in the wake of the storms along northern California beaches, the sun shone benignly. The surf, driven by those Pacific events, rode high and loud. And Monarch butterflies, orange and black, thousands of them, which had migrated from the Sierras to spend the winter on the temperate coast, flashed in the sunshine between rains, gliding through the blue air like Japanese kites or flights of birds. Truculent hummingbirds pursued each other, fought for territory around sweet-smelling bushes. The acacia popped into heady flower. Wild narcissus and calla lilies already bloomed along watercourses down the hills. Willow canes flamed red—the "burning bush"—while their buds, soft and velvet gray, emerged.

More rains will come to the Pacific Coast, more storms. Ships will get into trouble off San Francisco Light and off the Columbia Bar. Fishing boats will hole up in Bodega Bay, Tillamook Bay, Grays Harbor, and Willapa Bay. With great relief tankers and freighters will leave the ocean and enter the Strait of Juan de Fuca, the strait which Captain Cook missed, owing to bad weather, though he raised Cape Flattery, which he so named on the 22nd of March, 1778, "in token of the prospect of improvement of the weather which had for some days been very stormy."

But Spring will be on its way. Then the long dry Summer will begin. The fire will come in the Fall. Then the rains again, to put out the fire. That's the pattern of life in the Pacific States; and whether they are aware of it or not, everything and everybody that lives there subscribes to this design.